Herbert Spencer

Series Introduction

The *Major Conservative and Libertarian Thinkers* series aims to show that there is a rigorous, scholarly tradition of social and political thought that may be broadly described as 'conservative,' 'libertarian' or some combination of the two.

The series aims to show that conservatism is not simply a reaction against contemporary events, nor a privileging of intuitive thought over deductive reasoning; libertarianism is not simply an apology for unfettered capitalism or an attempt to justify a misguided atomistic concept of the individual. Rather, the thinkers in this series have developed coherent intellectual positions that are grounded in empirical reality and also founded upon serious philosophical reflection on the relationship between the individual and society, how the social institutions necessary for a free society are to be established and maintained, and the implications of the limits to human knowledge and certainty.

Each volume in the series presents a thinker's ideas in an accessible and cogent manner to provide an indispensable work for students with varying degrees of familiarity with the topic as well as more advanced scholars.

The following twenty volumes that make up the entire *Major Conservative and Libertarian Thinkers* series are written by international scholars and experts:

The Salamanca School by Andre Azevedo Alves (LSE, UK) and
  José Manuel Moreira (Universidade de Aveiro, Portugal)
Thomas Hobbes by R. E. R. Bunce (Cambridge, UK)
John Locke by Eric Mack (Tulane, UK)
David Hume by Christopher J. Berry (Glasgow, UK)
Adam Smith by James Otteson (Yeshiva, US)
Edmund Burke by Dennis O'Keeffe (Buckingham, UK)
Alexis de Tocqueville by Alan S. Kahan (Paris, France)
Herbert Spencer by Alberto Mingardi (Istituto Bruno Leoni, Italy)
Ludwig von Mises by Richard Ebeling (Northwood, US)

Joseph A. Schumpeter by John Medearis (Riverside, California, US)
F. A. Hayek by Adam Tebble (UCL, UK)
Michael Oakeshott by Edmund Neill (Oxford, UK)
Karl Popper by Phil Parvin (Loughborough, UK)
Ayn Rand by Mimi Gladstein (Texas, US)
Milton Friedman by William Ruger (Texas State, US)
Russell Kirk by John Pafford (Northwood, US)
James M. Buchanan by John Meadowcroft (King's College London, UK)
The Modern Papacy by Samuel Gregg (Acton Institute, US)
Murray Rothbard by Gerard Casey (UCD, Ireland)
Robert Nozick by Ralf Bader (St Andrews, UK)

Of course, in any series of this nature, choices have to be made as to which thinkers to include and which to leave out. Two of the thinkers in the series – F. A. Hayek and James M. Buchanan – have written explicit statements rejecting the label 'conservative.' Similarly, other thinkers, such as David Hume and Karl Popper, may be more accurately described as classical liberals than either conservatives or libertarians. But these thinkers have been included because a full appreciation of this particular tradition of thought would be impossible without their inclusion; conservative and libertarian thought cannot be fully understood without some knowledge of the intellectual contributions of Hume, Hayek, Popper and Buchanan, among others. While no list of conservative and libertarian thinkers can be perfect, then, it is hoped that the volumes in this series come as close as possible to providing a comprehensive account of the key contributors to this particular tradition.

John Meadowcroft
King's College London

Herbert Spencer

Alberto Mingardi

Major Conservative and Libertarian Thinkers

Series Editor: John Meadowcroft

BLOOMSBURY

NEW YORK • LONDON • NEW DELHI • SYDNEY

Bloomsbury Academic
An imprint of Bloomsbury Publishing Plc

1385 Broadway	50 Bedford Square
New York	London
NY 10018	WC1B 3DP
USA	UK

www.bloomsbury.com

Hardback edition first published in 2011 by the Continuum
International Publishing Group Inc.

This paperback edition published by Bloomsbury Academic 2013

Library of Congress Cataloging-in-Publication Data
A catalog record for this book is available from the Library of Congress.

ISBN: HB:	978-0-8264-2486-0
PB:	978-1-4411-6499-5
ePub:	978-1-6235-6482-7

Typeset by Newgen Imaging Systems Pvt Ltd, Chennai, India

Contents

Series Editor's Preface

Herbert Spencer was one of the foremost intellectuals of the Victorian era, his works widely read and debated by his contemporaries. But in the twentieth century Spencer's reputation suffered a dramatic decline, so that today his work is often seen as being of purely historical interest – an example of a particular mindset that has long been consigned to history.

In this book, Dr Alberto Mingardi of the Istituto Bruno Leoni makes a compelling case for the continued relevance and significance of Spencer's work. Spencer was a thinker who engaged with the big philosophical and practical issues of his day and ours: the relationship between the individual and the state; the nature of majoritarian democracy; the legitimacy of private property; the consequences of the transition from relatively simple, feudal communities to complex, industrial societies; and the causes of war and the prospects of international peace. In all these areas Spencer made important and original contributions that reward engagement with his work and ideas.

As Dr Mingardi sets out, Spencer's analysis of these issues makes him an important originator of the evolutionary classical liberal or libertarian approach that was exemplified in the twentieth century by F. A. Hayek. Much of Spencer's work develops the proposition that human civilization is on a progressive, evolutionary course towards a future in which government will provide only a minimal framework of the rule of law and the enforcement of property rights, allowing individuals to meet one another's needs in the marketplace. Hence, for Spencer, the future was individualist. But as the scope of state action expanded and classical liberal ideas became increasingly marginalised during the course of his life, Spencer grew evermore pessimistic about the future prospects for liberty.

By setting out Spencer's thought in a highly lucid and accessible manner, this volume makes a crucial contribution to the *Major Conservative and Libertarian Thinkers* series. It presents Spencer's intellectual contributions in the context of his life and times, considers the reception of Spencer's work by his contemporaries, notes its long decline in influence and argues for its continuing relevance to those scholars seeking to grapple with the proper relationship between the individual and the state. As such, this volume provides an excellent introduction to Spencer's work and engages with the more advanced debates that his thought addresses. Dr Mingardi shows that the neglect of Spencer by so many contemporary scholars has been to the detriment of political and social theory; Spencer is a scholar to be returned to the libertarian and conservative canon.

John Meadowcroft
King's College London

Acknowledgements

Most of this work is based upon my "Laurea" thesis, which I discussed at the University of Pavia in 2004 with Salvatore Veca and Ian Carter. They were the most benevolent and encouraging supervisors anyone could wish for. I am immensely grateful for the liberty they granted me.

Over the years, I have always benefited from the fatherly advice of Luigi Marco Bassani and Carlo Lottieri. My understanding, if any, of classical liberalism is deeply indebted to them.

This book would not have seen light if it hadn't been for John Meadowcroft. Special thanks are due to John not only for being so confident in me as to insist I take up the endeavour, but also for his patience with my many delays and weaknesses.

This book would have never been completed if it were not for the time spent at Franco Debenedetti's peaceful house in Dobbiaco, in the Dolomites. I am indebted to Franco for his patience with me, not to mention the many great conversations and glorious bottles of wine.

This book has many faults, for which I take sole responsibility. But it would have far more if my daily work as the director general of Istituto Bruno Leoni lacked the splendid aid of our executive team: Filippo Cavazzoni, Vera Costantino, Elena Lanzotti, Carlo Stagnaro, Sara Scordari. They are a crew of fabulous people, who make fighting for liberty a personal joy besides a moral duty. Oscar Giannino, as always, provided constant encouragement. David Perazzoni deserves more gratitude than I can express, for he patiently re-read every single sentence that escaped my pen. The corrections to the manuscript were completed during a period I spent as a Visiting Fellow at the Hoover

Institution (Stanford, California), where I benefited from a most hospitable environment.

This book is dedicated to the unforgettable memory of Lord Harris of High Cross, a Richard Cobden of our times.

1

Introduction

'The reports of my demise have been greatly exaggerated.'
Herbert Spencer (1820–1903) has long been considered nothing more than an archeological relic of the Victorian era. In
his classic *The Structure of Social Action* (itself now somehow a forgotten work), the great sociologist Talcott Parsons (1902–79)
claimed Spencer as a victim of the very God he constantly
preached: Evolution. It was 'the vengeance of . . . evolution'
which led to the 'evolution of scientific theory' and evidently
killed Herbert Spencer (Parsons 1937, p. 3).[1]

Parsons, himself a 'liberal' in the modern sense, was quoting
Crane Brinton's (1898–1968) *English Political Thought in the
Nineteenth Century*. Brinton defined Spencer as 'the intimate
confidant of a strange and rather unsatisfactory God, whom
he called the principle of Evolution. His God has betrayed him.
We have evolved beyond Spencer' (Brinton 1949, p. 227).

Brinton was surely echoing what many thought in the 1930s,
when he asked:

Who now reads Spencer? It is difficult for us to realize how
great a stir he made in the world. The *Synthetic Philosophy*
penetrated into many a bookshelf which held nothing else
quite so heavy. It lay beside the works of Buckle and Mill on
the shelf of every Englishman of a radical turn of mind. It
was read, discussed, fought over. And now it is a drug on the
second-hand market. (Brinton 1949, p. 226)

In a nutshell, it seems the fate of Herbert Spencer was very much the reverse of the destiny of Friedrich Wilhelm Nietzsche (1844–1900). Twenty years Spencer's junior, Nietzsche was not widely recognized in life but exerted a lasting influence on the development of twentieth-century thinking. On the other hand, Spencer was seen by his contemporaries as a major thinker for most of his adult life. Though his nervous breakdowns, poor health and idiosyncratic character seemingly did not allow him to enjoy this celebrity status, he was indeed discussed and much thought of by the educated man of his age. His popularity went beyond the boundaries of the Anglo-Saxon world as he developed a growing following in continental Europe. He was 'on the edge': he provided his readers with the impression that he was one of the very few masters dominating the intricacies of the time, and casting light on the obscurity of the future. There was hardly a subject he did not write on, and his *Synthetic Philosophy* seemed to embrace all the span of the knowable. He was perhaps the only philosopher to sell one million copies of his work while still alive. Robert Nisbet (1913–96) noted that

> his relentless rationalism, his unquenchable faith in the individual and in voluntary cooperation, and his conviction of the necessity in the entire world of human progress toward ever higher levels of freedom, gave him an influence in social and economic areas that has been exceeded only by Karl Marx. (Nisbet 1980, p. 236)

In a way, he was *the* philosopher of his time. 'If the Victorian age was pre-eminently the age of self-made men, Spencer was pre-eminently its self-made philosopher' (Taylor 2007, p. 144).

Alas, posterity can be a hard judge. The tides turned very rapidly for Spencer.

When the British people mourned his death in 1903, memorial activities were readily set up with no economies of pomp. Among others, 'a sum of £1000 was presented to the University of Oxford by Mr Shyamaij Krishnavarma to found a Herbert Spencer Lectureship' (Duncan 1904, II, p. 483). If Spencer would have approved of his friend Auberon Herbert (1838–1906) giving a lecture in this series in 1905 and Sir Francis Galton (1822–1911) delivering it in 1906, he would have been distinctly less pleased with many of the subsequent lecturers. His intellectual legacy was quickly dispersed, and looked irrelevant as the world moved towards more government intervention rather than less in the many areas of social life.

Talking of metaphors, the fate of Spencer is best epitomized by the fact that Beatrice Potter (1866–1943), the daughter of dear friends who grew up literally at his knee, turned out to be perhaps the most vocal and effective promoter of Fabian socialism, a set of ideas that Spencer identified as inimical to his own.

Therefore, it is hardly surprising that such an unforgiving dismissal of Spencer as Brinton's dates back to the New Deal era, when the events seemed destined to march in a very un-Spencerian direction. Herbert Spencer's political convictions were constants throughout his life. If he was attacked for minor self-corrections over the years, his consistency was remarkable. Ever since his youth, he preached the gospel of smaller government, believing that the evolution of human cooperation was leading us in the way of freedom. In his first, major work, *Social Statics*, he came to postulate 'the right to ignore the state.' Later in time, he stopped to bend over anarchism, but never surrendered to the idea that any step towards a bigger state could be anything less than a form of atavism. He was an adamant pacifist and must not have been pleased to see the first steps toward what later came to be the modern welfare state in Britain. In the face of rising public expenditure both on the 'social' and the 'military' front, he opposed the warfare–welfare state to the bone.

Very soon after history gave birth to the twentieth century, in England as well as in the United States as much as anywhere else in the world 'in the transition from war mood to the disillusionment of the 1920s, the philosophy and practice of liberalism was the chief victim' (Ekirch 2009, p. 243).

There are many reasons why Spencer could not be popular in the twentieth century. One was his adamant faith in the progress of human society 'from status to contract,' to quote Henry

Sumner Maine (1822–88), from archaic face-to-face societies
dominated by coercion to impersonal, freer societies driven by
private contracts. Mercilessly the day after day developments of
politics were contradicting the pattern of evolution he sketched
in all his writings: less spontaneous cooperation, and growing
coercion, seemed to be the inevitable consequences of progress.
As free markets did not enjoy great popularity for most of the
twentieth century, so one of their staunchest champions could
hardly enjoy much good press.

But Spencer was on the losing side in other fields too. The
ever-growing professionalization in academia and a higher
division of intellectual labour made it increasingly difficult for
scholars to cope with system-builders whose ambitions were as
great as Spencer's. Plus, the sticky label of 'social Darwinist' came
to cast an ominous shadow over his figure – social Darwinism
being associated with racism and imperialism. Also, the traditions
of natural rights and of classical utilitarianism, both influential
in the development of Spencer's thought, were long deemed as
vestiges of the past – at least until the 1970s, when they both
started to enjoy some kind of a revival.

Contrary to figures such as Darwin (1809–82) and Mill
(1806–73), it became fashionable to dismiss Spencer as at best
an ideologue. For such a distinguished historian of the Victorian
age as Gertrude Himmelfarb, he was nothing but 'an autodidact
and popularizer by temperament,' whose work was 'a parody of
philosophy' (Himmelfarb 1959, p. 213).

The man of his age, Spencer had difficulties in making it into
the future. But perhaps the question of who reads Spencer today
could, in the early twenty-first century, bear different answers
than it did right after the Great Depression.

A growing body of literature is now seeing the development of
the free society through evolutionary lenses. Though some of
these authors do not even quote Spencer (e.g. Rubin 2002), and
though they clearly can access a much wider pool of information
about our evolutionary past, they reach conclusions that are surprisingly similar to those that Spencer foresaw in the 1800s.

A caveat is due to the reader. This short monograph concen-
trates exclusively on Herbert Spencer's political thought, and

the much larger body of his work is examined only superficially and specifically in connection with his political thinking. Spencer produced four major works on political philosophy: *The Proper Sphere of Government* (1842–43), *Social Statics* (1851), *The Man Versus the State* (1884), and 'Justice,' the fourth part of his *Principles of Ethics* (published before the remaining parts, in 1891). This monograph will focus by and large on Spencer's political thought as it emerges from these works, plus a few important articles on political subjects. Frequent reference will be made to his *Autobiography* (1904) because in those two fat volumes Spencer reconstructs the development of his thought over his entire lifetime.

Spencer's life was not adventurous or by any standard filled with exciting events, but I have tried to summarize it, albeit very briefly, in the Chapter 2. The central chapter of the monograph aims to present, in a way that aims to be first and foremost fair to him, his political thought. I have chosen to discuss his influence by linking him directly to the work of some of his disciples and to later thinkers who – for the most part independently – have developed similar ideas. This is done in the last two chapters.

To present a great thinker's worldview synthetically is always a challenge – and Spencer is no exception. Since he wrote so extensively, it is very difficult to pretend to master his thinking to the most minute detail. System builders are often possessed by fundamental intuitions that they stretch to the limits in their overreaching analyses. I will necessarily present Spencer through his generalizations and his judgments, leaving aside the cornucopia of empirical considerations and little insights they are founded upon. Spencer is an incredibly rich and interesting author, I hope this book may succeed in conveying at least a small portion of such richness and interest to the reader.

Note

[1] In a perceptive debunk of Parsons, Lorenzo Infantino noted that the very opposite might be true: authors who 'did not adapt themselves to Parsons's plan' were intentionally trashed in his work. See Infantino 1998, pp. 132–3.

2

The Life and the Character

Family and Dissent

Born in Derby on 20 April 1820, Herbert Spencer took pride in emphasizing how he came to the world in a 'dissenting family.' Dissenters, or Nonconformists, were Protestants who did not belong to the established Church of England. In England, after the *Act of Uniformity* of 1662 a Nonconformist was an English subject belonging to a non-Christian religion or any non-Anglican church. People who advocated religious liberty may also have been more narrowly considered as such. Presbyterians, Congregationalists, Baptists, Quakers, and those less organized were considered Nonconformists at the time of the *Act of Uniformity*. Later, as other groups formed, the label applied to them as well. These latter included Methodists, Unitarians, and members of the Salvation Army.

In England, Nonconformists were restricted from many spheres of public life and were ineligible for many forms of public educational and social benefits until the repeal in 1828 of the *Test and Corporation Acts* and the subsequent toleration. For instance, attendance at an English university had required conformity to the Church of England before University College, London (UCL) was founded, compelling Nonconformists to fund their own dissenting academies privately. For this very reason, intellectuals as prominent as Spencer or the two Mills never made it to the universities of the day.

Not surprisingly, then, Dissent was one of the magnets in nine-teenth-century politics in England.[1] The disestablishment of the

Church of England was the centre around which all the other political fights for liberty came to gravitate: this most crucial of issues helped in keeping together a vast movement, rooted both in the bourgeoisie and the lower classes that campaigned for an extension of freedom, culminating in the repeal of the Corn Law in 1848.

Of most of the activists in this movement, it can be said – as it was of those 'plebeian Dissenters' who fought the odious tariffs on corn – that they 'shared a Puritan cultural background requiring high moral standards and stimulating political radicalism. Their conflict with the Anglican Church was mainly political and social and was rationally motivated, being the struggle of subordinated groups to achieve self-determination' (Biagini 1992, p. 15).

Herbert's father, George (1790–1866), was a Wesleyan Methodist who drifted to Quakerism and had a vigorous intellectual life. He ran a private academy, originally founded by his own father, and was involved with the Derby Philosophical Society founded by Erasmus Darwin (1731–1801). By contrast, his Uncle Thomas (1796–1858) was an Anglican clergyman who married an evangelic. Even though Thomas stayed within the Church of England, he had a strong personality, which led him to have quarrels with his bishop about his ideas on separation of church and state, and exerted a lasting influence on his nephew. According to Spencer, the 'spirit of Nonconformity' was somewhat naturally infused in his family, his uncle included. Mark Francis, however, in a recent thorough study of Spencer's life, has questioned this claim:[2] Francis (2007) notes that what Spencer calls 'nonconformity' is actually a superabundant exposure to paternal authority in his youth, which, according to him, had lasting consequences on the young Herbert.

What we know about Spencer's family comes mainly from his two volumes of *Autobiography (pub. 1904)* and from the work of the ever-loyal David Duncan (1839–1923), one of the assistants he employed in later years. We can only speculate whether Spencer was portraying his childhood to conceal the trauma of the overbearing paternal authority he was subjected to, or whether he wanted to paint himself as a dissenter from the general consensus right from the beginning of his life, or even whether his account is at all genuine. Whatever the facts of the case may be, we shall note that Spencer wanted to convey the notion that his relatives showed some 'pronounced family traits' (Spencer 1904, I, p. 11), and particularly 'the nonconformity tendency,' namely, 'the lack of regard for certain of the established authorities, and readiness to dissent from accepted opinions.'

This nonconformist tendency was not merely a form of dissatisfaction with or disengagement from the status quo. Spencer maintained that

> beyond the relative independence of nature thus displayed, there was a correlative dependence on something higher than legislative enactments. Under circumstances indicated by the bearing of persecution for religious beliefs, nonconformity to human authority implies conformity to something regarded as higher than human authority . . . there is obedience to regulations, upheld as superior to the regulations made by men.
> (ibidem)

Spencer seemed to believe that his family was made of many Antigones, whereas a modern understanding, like that of Francis, leads one to suspect that his father and uncle may have been more at ease playing Creon.

The chief trait of his childhood was, for Spencer, 'the disobedience' that was 'the correlative of irreverence for governing agencies' (Spencer, 1899, p. 305). Looking back at his life, Spencer seemed to be certain that 'this natural trait operated throughout life, tending to make me pay little attention to the established opinion on any matter which came up for judgement, and tending to leave me perfectly free to inquire without restraint' (Spencer 1899, p. 305). Still, there is but one proof of such a sense of rebellion in Spencer's childhood. This has to do with him running away from Hinton, where he was brought to study under his Uncle Thomas. Spencer resented the discipline and uncongenial studies and, at age thirteen, he decided to run 130 miles back home to Derby. His rebellion was promptly curbed and he was sent back to his uncle's house. In various letters (see, for example, Duncan 1908, I, pp. 21ff.), Thomas rejoiced at the young Herbert's manners becoming better with time and the fact that he gradually came to accept the uncle's authority.

Such an education may help in explaining why the other trait that Spencer saw in his family members and believed he was himself bound to replicate, was the attitude that 'proximate gratifications,' seen as small, 'are sacrificed to future gratifications which were conceived as relatively great' (Spencer 1904, I, p. 12).

This very principle came to influence deep down the development of Spencer's mature thought:

That the spirit of nonconformity is shown by me in various directions no one can deny: the disregard of authority, political religious, or social, is very conspicuous. Along with this there goes, in a transfigured form, a placing of principles having superhuman origins above rules having human origins; for throughout all writings of mine relating to the affairs of men, it is contended that ethical injunctions stand above legal injunctions. And once more, there is everywhere shown in my discussion of political questions, a contemplation of remote results rather than immediate results, joined with an insistence of the importance of the first as compared with that of the last. (Spencer 1904, I, pp. 12–13)

As we said, the relative whom Spencer came to know best was his Uncle Thomas. Thomas had studied at Cambridge: 'His successes were the results not of any unusual endowments but rather of a good memory and hard work' (Spencer 1904, I, p. 26).

Thomas turned out to be a very important figure for his nephew, for he provided him with access to a world of ideas and political agitations. Of him, we know that

> differing profoundly from those Church-of-England priests who think their duty consists in performing ceremonies, conducting praises, offering prayers, and uttering such injunctions as do not offend the influential members of their flocks, his conception of the clerical office was more like that of the old Hebrew prophets, who denounced the wrongdoings of both people and rulers. He held that it came within his function to expose political injustice and insist on equitable laws. (Spencer 1904, I, p. 29)

In particular, Thomas 'took an active part in the agitation for the repeal of the Corn Laws – attending meetings, giving lectures, writing tracts' (Spencer 1904, I, pp. 29–30). His role was so prominent that 'he said grace at the first Anti-Corn Law banquet' (Spencer 1904, I, p. 30). The influence Thomas had on his nephew was great and lasting – and permanently tuned him to the ideological *Zeitgeist* of his early years. This was the time when 'Free trade was the popular ticket in Britain at the time. People rallied to the defence of free trade as the keystone of democracy, peace, and prosperity' (Trentmann 2008, p. 3).

Upon his uncle's death, Herbert reluctantly wrote an obituary emphasizing how his uncle 'may be regarded as having presented in a high degree the predominant peculiarities of the Englishman.' He is described as showing 'an unusual proportion of that unflagging energy which is so distinctive of the race;' he was 'practical' in his thought and perseverant, and throughout his life, 'he exhibited a great amount of that English characteristic – independence' (Spencer 1904, I, p. 32). The predominant character of his uncle was, for young Herbert, 'a strong sense of justice,' which is what 'stimulated him to join in the Anti-Corn Law agitation' (Spencer 1904, I, p. 33).

The obituary written by the young Herbert reads like an affectionate eulogy to posterity but was seen as controversial by his contemporaries. Herbert stressed the judgemental attitude of his uncle, referring to his 'love of approbation' as 'overpredominant,' and he offered a truthful portrait of the strong and indeed difficult character of a person who had influenced him so much.

In his Uncle Thomas, his father George, and their brothers Henry and William, Spencer thought that 'certain marked traits were thus common to all the brothers. Individuality was very decided; and, as a consequence, they were all regarded as more or less eccentric' (Spencer 1904, I, p. 39).

The description of Spencer's parents was somehow ambiguous. Of his father, Spencer says that he was 'morally superior' to the brothers (including Thomas) and that 'Save in certain faculties specially adapting me to my work, inherited from him with increase, I consider myself as in many ways falling short of him, both intellectually and emotionally as well as physically' (Spencer 1904, I, p. 43).

George Spencer was a teacher 'from boyhood – beginning, I suppose, in his father's school: and he was not out of his boyhood when he gave private lessons' (Spencer 1904, I, p. 49). He established himself as a private teacher, working for prominent families in Derbyshire. Herbert somehow explicitly links his own, distinctive views on education to his father's 'natural tendency towards non-coercive treatment' (Spencer 1904, I, p. 50). Politically speaking, George Spencer was described by his son as 'a pronounced Whig or something more' (Spencer 1904, I, p. 47). He also took part in the anti-slavery agitations and 'has ever been deeply interested on the behalf of the Negros' (Spencer 1904, II, p. 139).

Admiration and loyalty to his father led Spencer to maintain a lifelong correspondence with him.[3] He had a great respect for his father's talents (he maintained that he would have made a first rate portrait painter; he would have made a great sculptor; and 'as an experimental investigator he would have been admirable'), but recognized that he was 'not kind to my mother' (Spencer 1904, I, p. 54).

As compared to his father and his uncle, we know little about Herbert's mother from his own voice. He acknowledged that she had an awkward relationship with his father and he presented her as somehow his intellectual inferior to an extent that made conversation and exchange of ideas, if not impossible, altogether difficult for sure. Still, Herbert refuses to hypothesize that love was lacking between the two of them. 'It was not that sympathy was absent, but it was habitually repressed in pursuance of fixed determinations' (Spencer 1904, I, p. 55). His father's care for his mother was observed to be greater in the later years – 'in the closing years of her life the solicitude about her was great' – and the difficulties are traced back to education, disappointment with the intellectual simplicity of his mother, and the 'chronic irritability consequent on his nervous disorder, which set in some two or three years after marriage and continued during the rest of his life.'

If, in respect of his father and his uncles, Spencer tries to underline what makes him similar to them, all of them being champions of Nonconformist free thinkers and committed eccentrics, in converse he says that his mother 'rather displayed an ingrained conformity' (Spencer 1904, I, p. 56). Although he acknowledges her life to have been 'less than enviable,' he is convinced that 'of my mother's intellect there is nothing special to be remarked.' She is said to be possessed of a 'sound judgment in the respect of ordinary affairs,' but at the very same time Spencer is certain that she never attempted to read 'my larger works which, if attempted, were promptly given up as incomprehensible. More humane words come when he remarks that 'the world may be divided into those who deserve little and get much and those who deserve much and get little. My mother belonged to the latter class; and it is a source of unceasing regret with me that I did not do more to prevent her inclusion in this class' (Spencer 1904, I, pp. 58–60).

Without entering psychoanalytical speculations, such a difficult relationship with his mother may count as an explanation for Spencer's complete lack of sexual intercourse with women in his adult life.[4]

Through family connection, the young Herbert entered his first job in the thriving railroad business (at the very peak of the 'railways mania'). Spencer found reasons for enjoyment and fulfilment in the job – 'there was scope for accuracy and neatness, to which I was naturally inclined' (Spencer 1904, I, p. 132) – and travelled the country by and large. For Spencer, 'they had been on the whole satisfactory years' (Spencer 1904, I, p. 189) but in 1840 he experienced 'a revival of an interest awakened during his boyhood at home and kept alive at Hinton. . . . As his prospects in engineering declined, the hereditary interest in man and society reasserted itself' (Duncan 1908, I, p. 367) – an interest that was indeed to shape his entire life.

The World of Letters and *The Economist*

Spencer's debut in the world of letters and politics came in 1842–43, when he published eleven letters in *The Nonconformist*, later to be collected under the title The Prosper Shere of Government. The journal was established to advocate the dissolution of the connection between church and state: 'the motto of the paper being a sentence from Burke, "The Dissidence of Dissent and the Protestantism of the Protestant religion"' (Spencer 1904, I, p. 237).[5]

The letters were immensely important for the development of Spencer's political thought, of which they remain one of the most vivid and beautiful examples. But they were not particularly helpful in sorting out a suitable way of earning a living. After leaving the railroad business, Spencer alternated collaborations with a variety of journals (*The Nonconformist* and similar outfits), a period as assistant editor of a small journal called *The Pilot*, some day-dreaming stretches about becoming an inventor, and the contemplation of the possibility of undertaking teaching as a job – none of this with great satisfaction. He even conceived the idea of setting up his own newspaper, *The Philosopher*, abandoning it quickly since he was unable to raise funds for such an endeavour. His life was to change when he received an offer of a position at *The Economist*. He was introduced to the editor, James Wilson (1805–60), through a letter written by his Uncle Thomas. We know that Spencer presented Wilson with a copy of *The Proper Sphere of Government*, which Wilson declared he sympathized with (Edwards 1993, p. 143). Wilson gave Spencer a job as the *subeditor* of *The Economist* and 'although the salary was low, free accommodation in a central location made the offer attractive' (Edwards 1993, p. 145).

On joining the magazine in 1848, Spencer was not particularly impressed. He knew he did not like the monotony of a routine job, being sure that in his case 'the advantages which intellectual freedom confers seem to have outweighed the disadvantages' (Spencer 1904, I, p. 337).

Still, the *Autobiography* suggests that Spencer liked the light workload and the fact that 'the period was one in which there was going on an active development of thought. There then germinated various ideas which unfolded in after years' (Spencer 1904, I, p. 424).

Ruth Dudley Edwards, the historian of the magazine, claims that '*The Economist* was far more important to Spencer than was Spencer to *The Economist.*' This claim may well be right. As Edwards explains, during all Spencer's stay at the magazine, 'he continued to limit himself to work that could have been done by anyone competent, and had attributed to him only one leading article . . . which made suggestions for improving the quality of London water' (Edwards 1993, p. 145).

Surely it can be said that at *The Economist* he found at least an important intellectual *comrade*: Thomas Hodgskin (1787–1869).

Hodgskin is a much neglected and indeed relevant figure. From Spencer's own writings, it is hard to glean to what extent Hodgskin may have had a lasting influence on the development of Spencer's thought. For one thing, Spencer always claimed originality. This was also the case vis-à-vis the conjecture that

Hodgskin exercised a lasting influence on him.[6] Hodgskin, a real self-made man of letters, led an adventurous and difficult life before joining *The Economist*, which can be certainly said to show to a higher degree those very same traits of rebellious radicalism Spencer admired so much.

Hodgskin was born in 1787 at Chatham in Kent, where his 'selfish, vain and spendthrift' (Halevy 1956, p. 29) father worked as a storekeeper in the naval dockyard, reducing the family to misery by spending his time and money at the tavern (Stack 1998, p. 35). At age of 12, his father found him a position on a warship as a naval cadet. He served during the Napoleonic Wars but his resentment of the harshness of naval discipline led him to an outburst against one of his superiors. Once retired, he completed his first book, *An Essay on Naval Discipline*. This essay drew the attention of the radical Francis Place (1771–1854) who took young Hodgskin under his wing and in turn introduced him to Jeremy Bentham (1748–1832) and James Mill (1773–1836).

From 1815, Hodgskin traveled the Continent, mostly by foot and in poverty, to study the policies of different governments. In 1820 he published a book entitled *Travels in the North of Germany*. In 1822 he obtained a job as parliamentary reporter for the London *Morning Chronicles*; then in 1823 he entered a variety of ventures aimed at providing instruction for men at mechanics' institutes. In 1825 he published *Labour Defended Against the Claims of Capital*; in 1827 *Popular Political Economy;* and in 1832 his major work, *The Natural and Artificial Right of Property Contrasted*.

Because he favoured the right of association for workers, typically signed his work under the nickname *A Labourer*, and championed the labour theory of value following John Locke (1632–1704) and Adam Smith (1703–90), Hodgskin has been commonly considered a proto-Marxist.[7] Still, his full-fledged individualism would lead us to consider him as a libertarian of the anarchist persuasion, convinced that since 'property is not regulated and determined by human laws . . . society can exist and prosper without the lawmaker, and consequently without the tax-gatherer' (Hodgskin 1832, p. 1). For Hodgskin, 'all law-making, except gradually and quietly to repeal all existing laws, is arrant humbug.'

In his most famous work, Hodgskin indeed produced a strong defence of the Lockean system against utilitarianism.

By joining *The Economist*, Hodgskin renounced personal literary pre-eminence to practise anonymous journalism (then, as today, one of the hallmarks of *The Economist*). For Ruth Dudley Edwards, the fact that Hodgskin was hired by editor James Wilson proved 'one of his [Wilson's] major gifts as an editor: he recruited exceptional talent' (Edwards 1993, p. 128). 'Hodgskin certainly added depth, scope and erudition to the literary pages along with a sharpness and combativeness that suited the paper's style.'

Between Spencer and Hodgskin, bonds of friendship developed easily. According to Edwards, 'Hodgskin . . . spent evenings with Spencer and took a deep interest in his projected book' (Edwards 1993, p. 146). Affection on the part of Hodgskin for the young Spencer is clear in his review of *Social Statics*, published in *The Economist* itself. Praising the talent he spotted, Hodgskin wrote that 'the author of the present work is no ordinary thinker, and no ordinary writer; and he gives us, in language that sparkles with beauties, and in reasoning at once novel and elaborate, precise and logical, a very comprehensive and complete exposition of the rights of men in society.' *Social Statics* was actually a title suggested by Hodgskin, who read the book as a draft, whereas Spencer originally fancied the idiosyncratic title of *Demostatics*.

Spencer left *The Economist* in 1853, after inheriting a £500 bequest from his uncle ('a considerable sum' that lessened the risks involved in living as an independent thinker), and he also endeavoured to take 'steps to extend my literary connexions' (Spencer 1904, I, p. 415). More than *The Economist*, the life at the magazine found him 'revelling in the new friendships that followed on the success of his book' (Edwards 1993, p. 150).

Particularly important was the acquaintance with *The Westminster Review*, which

had been an organ of genuine Liberalism – the Liberalism which seeks to extend men's liberties; not the modern perversion

of it which, while giving them nominal liberties in the shapes
of votes (which are but a means to an end) is busily decreasing
their liberties, both by the multiplication of restraints and
commands, and by taking away larger parts of their incomes to
be spent not as they individually like, but as public officials
like. (Spencer 1904, I, p. 421)

The *Westminster Review* was the radical competitor to the Whig
Edinburgh Review and to the Tory *Quarterly Review*. It was edited
by John Chapman (1821–94), a radical publisher who had developed an interest in Spencer and published *Social Statics*. Chapman's bookstore was opposite of *The Economist*'s offices, and
Chapman assembled around his persona an impressive number
of radical intellectuals. As noted by Michael Taylor, for Spencer
'the Chapman salon was both a substitute university education
and a surrogate senior common room' (Taylor 2007, p. 15).

George Eliot, Laurencina Potter, Beatrice Webb

In his house John Chapman had for a time a very special guest
who conquered a unique place in Herbert Spencer's heart.
Though Spencer didn't know it at the time, she also had an
affair with Chapman (who was married), and led an intense
love life.

Marian Evans (1819–80), known as an author with the nom de
plume, George Eliot, met Spencer for the first time 'about the
middle of 1851' and 'later in the same year he took Mr. Lewes to
call on her,' as the ever-loyal Duncan tells us (Duncan 1908, I,
p. 83). George Henry Lewes (1817–78), philosopher and critic,
was one of Spencer's literary acquaintances and was then to have
an open, scandalous affair with Evans.

The relationship between Spencer and Eliot has been under-
standably the matter of much speculation. 'The incidents of our
private lives often prove to us the fallibility of our judgments'
(Spencer 1904, I, p. 421), wrote Spencer, and in a way, meeting
Eliot was *the* incident of his private life.

In his *Autobiography* Spencer 'conceals' his love for her, constantly downplaying his sentiments (Francis 2007, pp. 57ff.). He portrays the time they spent together as largely a matter of chance, writing that 'my free admissions for two, to the theatres and to the Royal Italian Opera,[8] were, during these early months of 1852, much more used than they would otherwise have been, because I had frequently – indeed nearly always – the pleasure of her companionship' (Spencer 1904, I, p. 395).

Signs of love and true affection are visible under the fog Spencer diffuses to cover up his sentimental engagement. Of Eliot he writes that 'Striking by its owner when in repose, her face was remarkably transfigured by a smile. The smiles of many are signs of nothing more than amusement; but with her smile there was habitually mingled an expression of sympathy, either for the person smiled at or the person smiled with' (Spencer 1904, I, p. 395). Similarly, he emphasizes her 'contralto voice' and cannot hide his enjoyment of her intellectual curiosity and her inquisitive character. He is taken by 'a current of self-criticism being an habitual accompaniment of anything she was saying or doing' (Spencer 1904, I, p. 396), but pities 'her lack of self-confidence which led her, in those days, to resist my suggestion that she should write novels' (Spencer 1904, I, p. 398). This note can be perhaps be seen as *evidently hypocritical*: if he didn't make her the love of his life, he still claims credit for having brought her literary talent to the light of the day.

Spencer vigorously complains that 'there were reports that I was in love with her, and that we were about to be married. But neither of these reports was true' (Spencer 1904, I, p. 399) and makes them nothing more than an illegitimate inference from the fact they were frequently seen together. For Francis,

> The encounter with Eliot forced him to recognize his own failure in masculinity by confronting him with a woman who seemingly possessed every one of the personalized and curious collection of feminine virtues on which he had mused when imagining his ideal woman. (Francis 2007, p. 57)

He felt guilty for being unresponsive to her love on a physical level and

could feel no passion but only emptiness and pain. During their affair he suffered for many months feeling uncomfortable with his own unresponsiveness; then he took his true love and fobbed her off on his friend, the notoriously sensual and libidinous G. H. Lewes. (*ibidem*)

If Francis's account is unforgiving of Spencer's weaknesses, a more charitable explanation of his insensitivity may simply be that he didn't find her physically attractive.[9] What certainly can be said is that this never-celebrated love provided the only romantic episode in an apparently loveless life.

This may explain why, among the very few personal friendships he developed (another to be remembered is certainly the one with Thomas Huxley [1825–95]), the most relevant one was with Richard (1817–82) and Laurencina Potter (1821–82). The relationship he entertained with Laurencina somehow resembled his association with George Eliot, but without the threatening insecurities connected with the mere possibility of a physical engagement: she was, after all, a married lady, and, even more importantly, she was already married to a friend of his.

The Potter home was visited by many men of science, philosophy and politics, but 'the family's most intimate friend among Victorian intellectuals was Spencer' (Epstein North 1985, p. 35). Richard and Laurencina showed a very different attitude towards him. An entrepreneur and a supporter of the Tory Party, Richard Potter felt great affection for Spencer, but wasn't an admirer of his ideas: 'he would walk with him, he would fish with him, he would travel with him . . . but argue with him or read his books he would not' (Webb 1979, p. 28). Laurencina Potter, the daughter of a merchant, instead found in Spencer an ally with whom she could talk and argue in never-ending evening debates.

Beatrice Potter (1858–1943), later Webb, was the couple's eighth daughter. Her relationship to Spencer was an important and ambivalent one. Without a family of his own, Spencer felt none-theless 'some natural desire to be surrounded by boys and girls' (Spencer 1904, I, p. 497). Spencer acted as 'liberator' to all of the Potter daughters, taking them on nature hikes in woods and encouraging them to 'rebel to authority' and to the boredom and constraints of the classroom. But for Beatrice he played the unique role of first intellectual mentor.

As she wrote,

> It was the philosopher on the hearth who, alone among my elders . . . encouraged me in my lonely studies; who heard patiently and criticized kindly my untutored scribblings about Greek and German philosophers; who delighted and stimu-lated me with the remark that I was a "born metaphysician", and that I "reminded him of George Eliot" who was always pressing me to become a scientific worker. (Webb 1979, p. 28)

But of course Beatrice Potter was to join a cause very opposite to anything Spencer would hold dear, politically speaking. As Epstein North notes, 'she reacted vehemently against the Indi-vidualist ethic he shared with her mother;' she came to condemn his ' "failure to attain to the higher levels of conduct and feeling" and she eventually saw his warped personality as the sad result of the "bankruptcy of science when it attempts to realize the cause or the aim of human existence" ' (Epstein North 1985, pp. 35–6).

Nonetheless, Spencer, for her, was an educator and an initia-tor to the joys and problems of inquiries in social science. 'There is indeed no limit to what I owe to my thirty or forty years' intimacy with this unique life,' she recognized, 'no less as a warn-ing than as a model' (Webb 1979, p. 29).[10] The friendship between two persons of such a different age (Beatrice Potter being 38 years Spencer's junior) was still treasured by Beatrice Potter to the last, in spite of any disagreement, for having opened the gate to her intellectual career. 'As a little child,' she wrote, 'he was perhaps the only person who persistently cared for me – or rather who singled me out as one who was worthy of being trained and looked after' (Webb 1979, p. 38).

A Life of Books and Illness

By any standard, Herbert Spencer's life wouldn't make a great movie – he lived for his ideas, and so besides his ideas there is indeed little to report. After the publication of *The Principles of Psychology* in 1855, he engaged in a lifelong effort to put together his *Synthetic Philosophy* in serial form, with a new volume to be added every two years (but distributed in smaller instalments each quarter). It took him almost twice as long, and not because he spent too much time enjoying himself.

He made some travels abroad (including Egypt and relatively frequent forays to France and Italy), the effect of which was typically devastating on his self-reported health conditions. During most of his life Spencer suffered from a nervous ailment for which doctors could find no explanation. His *Autobiography* deals at length with his health problem, presenting the reader with the self-portrait of a hypochondriac. His life, however, does testify of a total dedication to the completion of his ambitious system – reading the *Autobiography* and the letters, one can sense the prospective of leaving his great system unfinished was a never-ending torment. He felt his project 'sufficiently extensive and onerous even for one in full health' (Spencer 1904, II, p. 32).

From 1856 he stopped living alone and resided with others, including families of various sorts. These cohabitations were of varying success, but gave him the worries and preoccupations of a somewhat nomadic life. He settled only in 1866, when he took a home at 37 Queen's Gardens, Lancaster Gate, London, with two lady guests.

In a recent work, Barry Werth (2009) built on Spencer's trip to America to explain the fascination of prominent Americans of the time with the idea of evolution. Spencer's travel to the United States was organized by Edward Youmans (1821–87), one of his most ardent followers and the publisher of a *Popular Science* magazine. Youmans was an active fund-raiser for Spencer, managing to take care of his relationship to publishers and to get money to keep him in the occupation of completing his system. At one point, to prevent the cessation of the publication of Spencer's works, Youmans raised some $7,000 and invested them in securities to the benefit of his favourite.

It was mainly because of Youmans's efforts that Spencer's works were 'published in England and America' and 'simultaneously published in France, Germany, Italy, Hungary and Russia' (Spencer 1904, II, p. 303).

Spencer's travel to America was memorable in many ways, not least for the tremendous distress it caused him. He ended up delivering only one speech, at a dinner at Delmonico's in November 1882. He was 'able to get through my prepared speech without difficulty, though not with much effect; for I have no natural gift of oratory, and what little power of impressive utterance' (Spencer 1904, II, p. 406). But the speech also surprised the audience because he engaged in 'a criticism of American life, as characterized by over-devotion to work' (ibidem).

An unwavering champion of the free market, Spencer was anyway convinced that

> life is not for work, but work is for life; and very often work, when it is carried to the extent of undermining life, or unduly absorbing life, is not praiseworthy but blameworthy. If we contemplate life at large in its ascending forms, we see that in the lowest creatures the energies are wholly absorbed in self-sustentation and sustentation of the race. Each improvement in organization, achieving some economy or other, makes the maintenance of life easier . . . The progress of mankind is, under one aspect, a means of liberating more and more life from mere toil. (Spencer 1904, I, p. 412)

His criticism of the 'gospel of work' not surprisingly 'baffled most of those who heard it' (Werth 2009, p. 281).

Spencer was one of the most widely appreciated thinkers of his time and a successful writer, but by no means an orator or a political activist. For most of his life, he avoided direct political action with the exemption of an unfruitful attempt to found an Anti-Aggression League in 1881. This was, in his words, 'a grievous mistake': the efforts came to nothing. He had only two social memberships that he seriously appreciated: the X Club – a small society of nine men who supported evolutionary theory and developed the habit of dining together in a sort of Darwinian Masonic lodge (Barton 1998) – and the Athenaeum Club, where membership was open only to very distinguished figures in the world of letters and arts (Spencer was admitted in the late 1860s).

Spencer never ceased to be intellectually active, virtually to the final moment (his very last book, *Facts and Comments*, a collection of articles, dates from 1902). He passed away on 8 December 1903, just a few days after he asked to see Beatrice Webb for the last time. Chronicles of the time (included in Duncan 1908, II, pp. 227 ff.) testify that his contemporaries were fully aware that the last of his kind had died: 'Societies at home and abroad vied with one another in their eagerness to pay a tribute to his memory. From Italy condolences were sent by both the government and the Chamber of Deputies' (Duncan 1908, II, p. 237). Money was donated for endowing a yearly lecture named after him at Oxford and commemorations popped up here and there. The notoriety of Spencer crossed oceans and continents, and it is staggering nowadays to grasp the extent of his fame. Still, he was promptly forgotten by posterity. One reason for this was the very ideas he preached, advanced, and held dear.

Notes

[1] The importance of religious struggles and toleration in the emergence of classical liberalism can seldom be underestimated. See, for example, Zagorin (2003).

[2] The particular situation of Thomas, which did not cause any disruption in the family but was accepted, his identity being somewhat a matter of choice, is one only of the many interesting arguments raised by Francis (2007).

[3] David Duncan notes that rare 'are the instances in which father and son have for over thirty years carried on their correspondence on such a high level of thought and sentiment' (Duncan 1908, I, p. 179).

4   Spencer's troubled relationship (or lack of) with women is examined by Francis (2007, pp. 51–68).

5   The reference is to a 1775 speech by Edmund Burke (1729–97), *On Conciliation with America*, in which he describes the 'religion most prevalent in our northern Colonies' as "a refinement on the principle of resistance; it is the dissidence of dissent and the Protestantism of the Protestant religion. This religion, under a variety of denominations, agreeing in nothing but in the communion of the spirit of liberty' (see Burke 1999, p. 240).

6   An exchange of letters on the subject, between Spencer and Hodgskin's widow saw Spencer explicitly writing, 'that he exercised any influence over my opinions I deny' (Spencer to Mary Hodgskin, 17 Apr. 1903). For two opposite interpretations of the exchange, see Francis (1978) and Stack (1998, pp. 189–93). Elie Halevy (1870–1937), in his book on Hodgskin, maintained the latter actually exercised a major influence on Spencer (1956, pp. 142 ff.).

7   The Webbs called Karl Marx 'Hodgskin's illustrious disciple' (1911, p. 147). Bertrand Russell (1872–1970), in his *A History of Western Philosophy*, labelled Hodgskin's work as 'the first Social rejoinder to Ricardo' (Spencer 2004, p. 704). Hutchinson considers such a mischaracterization to date back to Karl Marx, suggesting that 'Hodgskin would much more accurately be described as a "Smithian anarchist" than as a "Ricardian socialist" (Hutchinson 1978, p. 242 n.). In Halevy's words, 'Hodgskin always fought, on principle, against every intervention of the government and the law in the distribution of wealth, and . . . criticized the revenues of the landowner and the capitalist precisely because he attributed a legislative and governmental origin to them' (1956, p. 141).

8   Spencer appreciated music, and even occasionally wrote on the subject.

9   Taylor (2007, p. 16) points out that in his essay 'Personal Beauty' Spencer described physical traits resembling those of Eliot as the opposite of beauty. See 'Personal Beauty,' now in Spencer, *Essays: Scientific, Political, & Speculative*, 1891.

10 Beatrice Webb wrote at length on how she actually made use of Spencer's teachings in developing her worldview, so differently coloured, politically speaking. For example, she notes that 'the importance of functional adaptation was, for instance, at the basis of a good deal of the faith in collective regulation that I afterwards developed' (1979, p. 38).

3

Ideas

Free Trade and the Proper Sphere of Government

Herbert Spencer's Uncle Thomas, was deeply involved with the Anti-Corn Law League. He published essays whose titles included: 'The Prayer Book Opposed to the Corn Laws;' 'The Repeal of the Corn Laws, A Religious Question;' and 'The Anti-Corn Law Grace.' His nephew was likewise pervaded by a sincere enthusiasm for the Anti-Corn Law movement, as is crystal clear from his very first political tract in 1842–3, in the form of twelve letters sent to *The Nonconformist,* a weekly newspaper edited and founded by Edward Miall (1809–81).[1]

These letters still stand as an admirably synthetic exposition of the key principles and ideas of that doctrine that we could define as 'classical liberalism' – and that was referred to at the time as 'individualism.' This school of thought was sometimes designated as the Manchester School, a somewhat incorrect label that came to be used to dismiss its contributions.

A few words of clarification might be needed. The reference to *classical* liberalism is meant to distinguish it from 'modern' liberalism' – or, as it came to be known at the time of Spencer, 'new' liberalism. This is required because of a change in the meaning of the word 'liberalism,' deemed by economist Joseph A. Schumpeter (1883–1950) as a 'corruption' of the word. For Schumpeter,

As it developed in the late eighteenth and early nineteenth centuries, the intellectual movement that went under the name of liberalism emphasized freedom as the ultimate goal and the individual as the ultimate entity in the society. It supported *laissez-faire* at home as a means of reducing the role of the state in economic affairs and thereby enlarging the role of the individual; it supported free trade abroad as a means of linking the nations of the world together peacefully and democratically. But, beginning in the late nineteenth century, and especially after 1930 in the United States, the term liberalism came to be associated with a very different emphasis, particularly in economic policy. It came to be associated with a readiness to rely primarily on the state rather than on private voluntary arrangements to achieve objectives regarded as desirable. The catchwords became welfare and equality rather than freedom. In the name of welfare and equality, the twentieth-century liberal has come to favor a revival of the very policies of state intervention and paternalism against which classical liberalism fought. (Schumpeter 1954, p. 394)

To the corruption of 'liberalism,' Spencer himself devoted one of his most persuasive essays, 'The New Toryism,' in *Man Versus the State* (1881).

Classical liberalism can thus be understood as basically concerned with 'reducing the role of the state in economic affairs and thereby enlarging the role of the individual.' David Conway observes that

At bottom, what distinguishes from all others that form of societal order which classical liberals maintain best for all human beings is the magnitude of the measure of liberty which it accords its sane adult members. This form of polity uniquely grants them the liberty to do whatever they want, provided no one – but, at most, themselves – is harmed by their doing it. (Conway 1995, p. 8)[2]

To further clarify the concept, it is well worth noting, with Ralph Raico, that

Classical liberalism is based on the conception of civil society as, by and large, sell-regulating when its members are free to act within very wide bounds of their individual rights. Among these, the right to private property, including freedom of contract and free disposition of one's own labor, is given a very high priority. Historically, liberalism has manifested a hostility to state action, which, it insists, should be reduced to a minimum. (Raico 1995, p. 3)

Classical liberalism was basically the political philosophy Spencer learnt to appreciate in his youth – and stuck with all his life. During his formative years, Spencer could witness this very philosophy overcoming evermore imposing hurdles in public opinion, reaching an impressive political victory with the abolition of the tariffs on imported corn. 'Free trade' seemed to be an idea whose time had come.[3] The arguments developed by Adam Smith made their way in public opinion when a pair of passionate agitators, Richard Cobden (1804–65) and John Bright (1811–89), carried the message to the country and ultimately to Prime Minister Robert Peel (1788–1850), who took the decisive steps to abolish the Corn Laws in the aftermath of the Irish potato famine.[4]

What they accomplished turned out to be truly unique in history. As Frank Trentmann points out, in an era when the future of mass politics was heralded by the emergence of nationalism, Britain's free trade

created its own national story of liberation in which Free Traders had led Britons from hunger and bondage to food and freedom. The willingness to live in an open world, rather than follow a beggar-thy-neighbour drift towards tariffs and greater self-sufficiency, also followed from a more positive, democratic embrace of the consumer. (Trentmann 2008, p. 16)

Free trade 'put the consumer on the political map' at the same time that other European states were experimenting with a very different *première* of mass politics.

Cobden and Bright succeeded in very special circumstances, but they shared a world view that went beyond the state of affairs of their times. As it was noted,

> The school which Cobden . . . strengthened, affirmed that freedom was the natural condition of the individual, and that restraint must always be justified in order to be defended. In the presence of an outrageous and ruinous wrong, the old Corn Law, it assailed the principle of protection to agriculture with irresistible force. But it was the accident of a fact which caused the assault to be made on this position. It attacked every kind of protection, on the ground that the assistance given to one interest was an injury, a restraint, an indefensible control on other interests, which were depressed, impoverished, and dwarfed in consequence. The promoters of this doctrine knew very well that the orderliness and control which law imposes are the guarantees of personal liberty; but they understood by the beneficent operation of law that government or order which protects all equally, not that which gives a licence or advantage to a few at the expense of the rest of society. Every man is benefited by the police of justice, a section only is benefited by privilege. (Rogers 1873, p. x)

The Corn Laws were repealed in 1846. In fact, Spencer wrote and published *The Proper Sphere of Government* in 1842–43; he entered *The Economist* in 1848; *Social Statics* saw the light in 1851 when its author had already been introduced to the circle of intellectuals around John Chapman and to Thomas Hodgskin. Spencer was no leader of the Anti-Corn Law movement – but this was the air that he was breathing.

'Tapas' of Synthetic Philosophy

In his classic treatment of the subject, Albert V. Dicey (1835–1922) understands the triumph of individualism in England as the historic victory of 'Benthamism,' which in his opinion exerted a significant influence on lawmaking in the period 1825–70. Jeremy Bentham was indeed a towering intellectual figure of the period – but prominent liberals could take different routes indeed.

Spencer's intellectual journey was marked from the beginning by very different ambitions. A few words should be spent here on the core of his philosophy, besides politics – at least in general terms. Spencer's *Synthetic Philosophy* is a grandiose attempt in system building, that cannot be the object of a properly thorough analysis in these pages. However it is worth the reader's while to spend a few moments on this subject to frame Spencer's approach in its complexity. Spencer could be said to uphold a theory in which the freedom of the individual was the ultimate goal of social evolution: his ambitions as a political thinker fit with his larger ambitions as a philosopher.

In his *Autobiography* Spencer explains that he 'early became possessed by the idea of causation,' learning from his father that 'natural causation [is] everywhere operating' (1904, II, p. 6). Building on this insight, George H. Smith has persuasively argued that Spencer's work cannot be properly understood if his 'theory of causation' is not considered as the central tenet of his thought (Smith 1981).[5] This insight is key to understanding why Spencer's theory is really so *unitary*, covering social phenomena and natural phenomena alike.

In his *First Principles* (1862), Spencer explains that the universe is evolving towards increased complexity. The more it evolves, the more the universe relentlessly subdivides itself into evermore intricate aggregates. These aggregates themselves become more and more differentiated. The parts they are constituted of become increasingly dissimilar one from the other as the aggregates themselves become more and more heterogeneous. This trend towards heterogeneity is at the root of Spencer's law of cosmic evolution: 'Evolution is an integration of matter and concomitant dissipation of motion, during which the matter passes from an indefinite, incoherent homogeneity to a definite, coherent heterogeneity, and during which the retained motion undergoes a parallel transformation' (1915, p. 321). Not surprisingly, it has been remarked that 'it was physics, not biology, that represented the ultimate model of scientific certainty in Spencer's eyes' (La Vergata 1995, p. 197). 'Spencer's theory of evolution is primarily cosmological, not biological' (Smith 1978).

Spencer's cosmos entails a process of continuous change and adaptation, constituting an advance from homogeneity of structure to heterogeneity of structure. This was

> the law of all progress. Whether it be in the development of the Earth, in the development of life upon its surface, in the development of society, of government, of manufactures, of commerce, of language, literature, science, art, this same evolution of the simple into the complex, through successive differentiations, holds throughout. (Spencer 1857, p. 10)

As Michael Taylor noted, he 'aimed at nothing less than a mechanical interpretation of the universe in which every event could be explained in terms of the relations of cause and effect between incident forces' (Taylor 1992, p. 77).

In his paramount essay, 'Progress: Its Law and Cause,' Spencer was applying the 'law of progress' to a variety of examples: from the 'nebular hypothesis' to the evolution of language. The idea behind all Spencer's arguments is that somehow homogeneity is inherently unstable, whereas reaching a more sustainable equilibrium requires a continuous process of adaptation. This very 'equilibration' is put in motion by the need for the different parts of an organism to be better suited to the special conditions to which they are subjected. For Spencer, life is 'the continuous adjustment of internal relations to external relations' (1855, p. 375). There is a principle of the persistence of force (the principle of the conservation of energy): the impact of incidental forces makes homogenous phenomena less so and more heterogeneous by the virtues of adaptation. Any organism struggles to adapt to the external environment. 'Advance in integration being accompanied by advance in heterogeneity.' The cosmos is inevitably evolving, and all inorganic and organic phenomena are ever becoming more integrated, more specialized[6] and heterogeneous. This process is fuelled by the principle of 'the persistence of force,' from which, as Smith noted, 'follows the persistence of relations among forces' (Smith 1981, p. 124).

According to Smith, 'A theory of evolution is but the logical unpacking of the causal relations implicit within the persistence of force . . . if evolutionary laws are logically deducible from the persistence of force and the uniformity of law, then they should apply to all phenomena – from the inorganic to the super-organic (i.e. social phenomena)' (Smith 1981, p. 125).

Spencer is often mocked as the first social Darwinist, typically by those unfamiliar with his work – or on the contrary he is considered a Lamarckian, mostly in the attempt to dissociate his thinking from Darwin's. If great attention has been devoted to the fact he actually coined the fortunate expression 'survival of the fittest' – widely used to qualify the Darwinian concept of 'natural selection' – the notion of 'natural selection' was but a component of his evolutionary view. In his system Spencer found room both for 'the changes produced by functional adaptation . . . and the changes produced by "natural selection"' as one and the other resulting 'from the redistribution of matter and motion everywhere and always going on' (Spencer 1904, II, p. 100). He acknowledged that before Darwin's *Origin of the Species*, he 'ascribed all modification to direct adaptation to changing conditions; and was unconscious that in absence of that indirect adaptation effected by the natural selection of favourable variations, the explanation left the large part of the facts unaccounted for' (Spencer 1904, I, p. 502). Spencer's theory was 'neither Darwinian nor Lamarckian, although both Lamarckian and Darwinian factors can be seen to have been incorporated in the theory of evolution which he propounded' (Taylor 1992, p. 76).

What is true is that, vis-à-vis the Darwinians, Spencer keep insisting that survival of the fittest and direct adaptation were integrated processes that were combined in the dynamics of progress and evolution. 'The survival of the fittest must nearly always further the production of modifications which produce fitness, whether they be incidental modifications, or modifications caused by direct adaptation' (1864–67, I, 455).

This notion must always be kept in mind to better understand Spencer's social theory as well. One puzzling factor, for many commentators, is the fact that Spencer's fame as one of the founders of sociology rests by and large on his concept of a 'social organism.' The notion that there are certain basic similarities of structure and function between societies and biological organisms is clearly based on Spencer's evolutionary theory. Both societies and organisms were understood by Spencer as aggregates which can exist for a much longer time than their components, undergoing a process of evolution in which their structures develop through multiplication and differentiations. Differentiation, in Spencer's evolutionary theory, stems from a progressive specialization of functions: a process akin to the social division of labour.

In the light of his uncompromising individualism, the fact that Spencer used the metaphor of a 'social organism' was used either to charge him with some deep theoretical incongruities, or for using Spencerian bricks, so to say, to build a socialist-leaning edifice. If ambiguities have frequently been underlined by various commentators, Spencer nonetheless seemed to be very clear that his metaphor of the social organism did not imply he was drawing back from his individualism. Michael Taylor aptly remarked that 'Spencer avoided the collectivist implications of the organic analogy by employing it in a quite limited and specific sense' (Taylor 1992, p. 165). This point was highlighted also by Bruno Leoni (1913–67) who distinguished 'the use of the social organism analogy' in the individual thinkers from that in the organicists, by saying that 'the first, in striking contrast with the latter, see an ineliminable heterogeneity between the concept of society and the concept of the individual' (Leoni 2008, p. 137). In his essay on 'The Social Organism' Spencer explicitly states that

We have . . . a tolerably decided contrast between bodies – politic and individual bodies; . . . It is well that the lives of all parts of an animal should be merged in the life of the whole, because the whole has a corporate consciousness capable of happiness or misery. But it is not so with a society; since its living units do not and cannot lose individual consciousness, and since the community as a whole has no corporate consciousness. This is an everlasting reason why the welfare of the citizens cannot be sacrificed to some supposed benefit of the State, and why, on the other hand, the State is to be maintained solely to the benefit of citizens. The corporate life must here be subservient to the lives of the parts, instead of the lives of the parts being subservient to the corporate life. (Spencer 1860, I, p. 277)

That same essay begins with a favourable quotation of Sir James Macintosh (1765–1832) who 'got great credit for the saying that "constitutions are not made, but grow" . . . that societies are not artificially put together, is a truth so manifest that it seems wonderful men should ever have overlooked it' (Spencer 1860, I, pp. 265, 266). The metaphor of the social organism was used by Spencer to explain that 'society is a growth and not a manufacture.' This profound distrust of social engineering brings together Spencer with the Scottish Enlightenment thinkers and, among contemporary authors, with the other great liberal champion of evolutionism, Friedrich von Hayek (1899–1992).[7] As in Hayek's case, Spencer's individualism was founded on an understanding that 'society is made up of individuals; all that is done in society is done by the combined actions of individuals; and therefore, in individual actions only can be found the solution of social phenomena' (1855b, p. 29).

Spencer explained himself very well in an 1893 letter, by emphasizing that 'two things . . . are not at all to be identified – social cooperation and state interference' (quoted in Duncan 1908, II, p. 59). Individualism is not opposed to the existence of a social body, because 'it may and does go along with an

elaborate form of mutual dependence.' A collectivist reading
of his 'social organism' analogy may simply be the consequence
of a failure to distinguish, as Spencer so clearly did, between
government (the state) and society.

The social organism metaphor ultimately served Spencer's
purpose to explain that the evolution of societies followed a
similar path to the evolution of individual beings: from homo-
geneous to heterogeneous, from simple to complex.

These notes are by no means exhaustive – they are 'tapas' of
Spencer's synthetic philosophy, as required to approach the
plat du jour of this monograph, his political work. Writing in his
Autobiography on his first – and often considered juvenile – political tract, *The Proper Sphere of Government*, Spencer remarked with
the benefit of hindsight that there was 'the same belief in the
conformity of social phenomena to invariable laws; the same
belief in human progression as determined by such laws; the
same belief in the moral modification of men as caused by social
discipline; the same belief in the tendency of social arrangements of themselves to assume a condition of stable equilibrium'
(Spencer 1904, I, p. 137 n.).

We can already see why Robert Nisbet proclaimed that

without question, Herbert Spencer was the supreme embodi-
ment in the late nineteenth century of both liberal individualism and the idea of progress. No one before or since so
effectively united the two philosophies of freedom and progress, or so completely anchored the former in the latter. (Nisbet
1980, p. 229)[8]

The following pages will be devoted to a survey of the philosophy of freedom, anchored in the philosophy of progress briefly
examined so far.

Spencer's Early Dabbling with Political Philosophy

Spencer's career as a political thinker started, as described earlier, with the letters sent to *The Nonconformist* in 1842, which

resulted in the pamphlet, *The Proper Sphere of Government,* a text imbued by a great 'hostility to state action.' This is apparent in the very title: the *proper* sphere of government implies indeed an indictment of the *improper* one. These twelve letters (eleven plus one summarizing the different arguments) can aptly be considered a small classic in the history of classical liberalism (or individualism), for they are a crystal-clear exposition of the core principles of this doctrine. But to the student of Spencer, they have also a special interest because, though a juvenile work, they already exhibit a number of traits that would characterize Spencer's thinking to the end of his days (Peel 1971, p. 65).

For this reason, we will examine here *The Proper Sphere of Government* in detail and with particular attention. It may appear incongruous to devote such a long treatment to such a slim volume, but in fact we can think of *The Proper Sphere* as a representative précis of Spencer's evolving ideas.

The Proper Sphere of Government is written in the language of nonconformity and in the language of Lockean liberalism, with a strong emphasis on the concept of individual rights. It therefore does not display a consistent theory of evolution, whereas it is clear that some of its seeds are already planted. If the term 'evolution' only appears in Spencer's work after the publication of *Social Statics,* the idea of progress nevertheless dominates his earlier works too.

The first of the letters is succinct but revealing. Here, Spencer outlines the general framework of his system. The search for a general theory – a theory of causation – is apparent in Spencer right from the beginning. He writes:

Everything in nature has its laws. Inorganic matter has its dynamical properties, its chemical affinities; organic matter, more complex, more easily destroyed, has also its governing principles. As with matter in its integral form, so with matter in its aggregate; animate beings have their laws, as well as the material, from which they are derived. Man, as an animate being, has functions to perform, and has organs for performing those instincts; and, so long as he performs those functions,

as he obeys those instincts, as he bends to the laws of his
nature, so long does he remain in health. All disobedience to
these dictates, all transgression, produces its own punishment.
(Spencer 1843, p. 183)

A state of nature of 'men living together without any recognized laws' is described in vaguely Hobbesian terms, but then
Spencer adopts a Lockean two-stage vision of social contract:
the first, establishing society with rules; the second, setting up a
government properly understood.

The weak – those who have the least strength, or the least
influence – are oppressed by the more powerful: these, in
their turn, experience the tyranny of men still higher in the
scale; and even the most influential, are subject to the combined vengeance of those whom they have injured. (Spencer
1843, p. 185)

This latter fact (that the strongest could be the subject of the
combined vengeance of people they injured) explains why.

Every man, therefore, soon comes to the conclusion, that his
individual interest as well as that of the community at large,
will best be served by entering into some common bond of
protection: all agree to become amenable to the decisions
of their fellows, and to obey certain general arrangements.
Gradually the population increases, their disputes become
more numerous, and they find that it will be more convenient
to depute this arbitrative power, to one or more individuals,
who shall be maintained by the rest, in consideration of
their time being devoted to the business of the public. Here
we have a government springing naturally out of the requirements of the community. But what are those requirements?
(ibidem)

For Spencer, a government is needed, but

> not to regulate commerce; not to educate the people; not to
> teach religion; not to administer charity; not to make roads
> and railways; but simply to defend the natural rights of man –
> to protect person and property – to prevent the aggressions of
> the powerful upon the weak – in a word, to administer justice.
> This is the natural, the original, office of a government. It was
> not intended to do less: it ought not to be allowed to do more.
> (Spencer 1843, p. 187)

A government strictly limited to the administration of justice,
basically an agency that doesn't go beyond the functions of the
judiciary and the police, is the only one that could be considered
legitimate. Spencer understood that this was a narrow definition,
and thought that its strength was built on this very narrowness. He
rejected notions such as the one that government is founded for
the sake of the common good, because he thought the common
good to be too vague a concept to bear any concrete possibility of
implementation. Likewise, he defined 'justice' as comprehending
'only the preservation of man's natural rights. Injustice implies a
violation of those rights' (Spencer 1843, p. 188).

In the other letters, Spencer deductively derives a political
program on the premises he previously stated. The second letter
deals with the Corn Laws and the separation of church and state.
On the Corn Laws, he maintains that it is

> clear [that] we should never have had any corn laws; and, as
> the test may be applied to all other cases of restrictions upon
> commerce with a similar result, it is equally evident, that upon
> the same assumption, we should always have had free trade.
> (Spencer 1843, p. 189)

Similarly,

> An established church is not only unnecessary to the preserva-
> tion of the natural rights of man, but that inasmuch as it denies

the subject the 'rights of conscience,' and compels him to contribute towards the spread of doctrines of which he does not approve, it is absolutely inimical to them. So that a state, in setting up a national religion, stands in the anomalous position of a transgressor of those very rights that it was instituted to defend. It is evident, therefore, that the restrictive principle, would never have permitted the establishment of a state church. (Spencer 1843, pp. 190–1)

The third letter deals with the Poor Law system, arguing against it, on the grounds that it

> divides the community into two great classes – labourers and paupers, the one doing nothing towards the production of the general stock of food and clothing, and the other having to provide for the consumption of both. Hence it is evident that each member of the producing class, is injured by the appropriation of a portion of the general stock by the non-producing class. (Spencer 1843, p. 193)

This kind of statement may read as blatantly anti-solidaristic today, but in a society that came to celebrate thrift as proof of character, Spencer was certainly not playing the advocate of the great and plentiful. On the contrary, he was invoking the abolition of the Poor Law because he saw that, as far as public charity was concerned, 'the greater portion of it comes from the toils of the labouring classes.'

Moreover, campaigning for freer trade was 'the necessary consequence of the same principle that excludes a poor law' (Spencer 1843, p. 195), namely, that the state's duties are bound to be strictly limited, but the argument had, so to say, the same constituency, namely, the productive classes (including labouring and lower classes) that opposed both protectionism and the growing burden of compulsory benevolence.

The subsequent letter builds on the attack on the Poor Law, aiming to generalize it and develop more general principles.

For one thing, Spencer explains that he opposes the Poor Law insofar as it reduces the strength of society's self-protection system against individual misconduct. Poverty is a matter of chance, but not only so. Destitution can be the result of inappropriate conduct. Society rewards thrift and punishes laziness. By feeding the undeserving 'it not only takes away the punishment, but it also destroys the most powerful incentive to reformation. Adversity is, in many cases, the only efficient school for the transgressor.' The system of retribution in a free market is not perfect, but it is better than anything that might result from distorting its set of incentives.

From this somewhat empirical point Spencer moves to a theoretical justification of property. Private property is not 'a conventionalism,' but it 'follows, therefore, from the law of expediency directly, from the constitution of man directly, and from the revealed will of God by implication, that property is not a conventional, but a natural, institution.'

Property is expedient, because it sets the correct incentive for economic growth:

> Man's happiness greatly depends upon the satisfaction of his temporal wants. The fruits of the earth are a necessary means of satisfying those wants. Those fruits can never be produced in abundance without cultivation. That cultivation will never prevail without the stimulus of certain possession. No man will sow when others may reap. (Spencer 1843, p. 205)

But furthermore, property is a natural institution and derived from the will of God. Man's desire to possess, to accumulate property, proves that the nature of human beings implies the need for property rights. Being natural, property is also consistent with the biblical message. Since God 'wills the happiness of man' and 'happiness depends upon the fulfilment of certain conditions . . . he gives him laws, by obeying which he satisfies those conditions. . . The single command, "Thou shalt not steal", carries with it a complete charter of the rights of possession' (Spencer 1843, p. 208).

If Spencer's position on property rights was to become more nuanced in *Social Statics*, the fifth letter brings us to a subject that will always be central in his thinking: war. He writes that

> War has been the source of the greatest of England's burdens. Our landowners would probably never have dared to enact the Corn Laws had not the people been intoxicated by the seeming prosperity arising from war. The national debt, with all its direful consequences, would not have been in existence, had our rulers been deprived of the power of going to war. Our country would never have been drained of the hard earnings of her industrious sons, had not the uncurbed ambition of the aristocracy involved us in war. Capital that would have constructed all our railways many times over – that would have given every facility to commerce – that would have set it upon a real instead of a nominal foundation – property, the accumulated labour of generations, the grand national store in time of need, is gone forever. (Spencer 1843, p. 211)

War is the quintessential social tragedy and it does not 'invigorate the social organism' as some authors may maintain.[9] For Spencer, the notion that war may have positive social benefits was never contemplated – both for humanitarian and economic reasons.

Speaking on the influence of war on social life, he denounced with great passion the very idea that war can be conducive to greater social welfare, as the mobilization of public resources 'stimulates' the national product. War

> acts upon a nation, as wine does upon a man. It creates the same unnatural activity – the same appearance of increased strength. In a similar manner does it call forth the supplies of life and energy provided for the future; in like fashion is the excitement followed by a corresponding depression; and so

likewise is the strength of the constitution gradually undermined; and the short-sighted politician, who, judging by the
apparent prosperity it produces, pronounces war a benefit to
a nation, is falling into the same error as the man who con-
cludes that a spirituous stimulant is permanently strengthen-
ing, because he experiences an accession of vigour whilst
under its influence. (Spencer 1843, p. 212)

But, besides the artificial stimulation of the economic world, war
was to be repudiated because it hindered the development of
the relationship of mutual exchange and cooperation among
different societies.

War has been the nurse of the feudal spirit, so long the curse
of all nations; and from that spirit has flowed much of the
selfish and tyrannical legislation under which we have so long
groaned. If, for the last four or five centuries, the civilised
world, instead of having been engaged in invasions and con-
quests, had directed its attention to the real sources of
wealth – industry and commerce, science and the arts – long
since would our nobility have found that they were mere
drones in the hive, and long since would they have ceased to
glory in their shame. (Spencer 1843, p. 212)

From the beginning of his career Spencer was a pacifist – but
never of the utopian sort. He accepted defensive wars as necessary evils, exactly because 'the feudal spirit' was still nurtured
all over the world. Rightly, he understood that condemning
warfare in general and wars of conquest in particular was not
inconsistent with granting the state the duty of defending its
citizens from aggression.

If nations confined the attention of their governments to the
administration of justice, aggressive war would cease; but when
aggressive war ceases, defensive war becomes unnecessary. We
see, therefore, that the concession that it might be requisite

for the state to interfere in cases of invasion, implies no error in the definition. (Spencer 1843, p. 216)

The sixth letter builds on this strong rebuttal of war to denounce imperialism ('What would the colonies do without our governance and protection? I think facts will bear me out in replying: Far better than they do with them' [Spencer 1843, p. 217]). This is another theme that Spencer did not abandon throughout his life.

Spencer opposed colonialism and special trade regimes as benefiting only 'the monopolists' whom he identified with 'the aristocracy.' But he furthermore used both economics-related ('the riches of a country are not increased by great colonial possession') and humanitarian arguments against the imperial state ('if emigration was carried on by private enterprise, the aborigines would obviously be less liable to the unjust treatment, which has ever characterised the conduct of civilised settlers towards them' (Spencer 1843, p. 222). Richard Cobden was also an ardent pacifist who campaigned against the Crimean War and the expansion of militarism. The new science, economics, recommended trade and not conquest: an aggressive view of the state was typical of the mercantilists, whereas free traders preached peace.

In the seventh letter, Spencer anticipated another of his recurrent interests: education. He wrote, 'A system of national instruction cannot be comprehended under the administration of justice.' For one thing, national education will almost by definition mean the imposition of uniformity in society by harmonizing attitudes and beliefs via teaching.

Natures differently constituted must be gradually brought, by its action, into a condition of similarity. The same influences, working upon successive generations, would presently produce an approximation to a national model. All men would begin to think in the same direction – to form similar opinions upon every subject. One universal bias would affect the mind of society; and, instead of a continual approach to the truth, there would be a gradual divergence from it. (Spencer 1843, p. 230)[10]

Not that Spencer was necessarily a conservative defender of the more or less *laissez-faire* education system of his time, but he thought that

under our present condition, the eccentricities and prejudices induced by one course of education, are neutralised by the opposing tendencies implanted by others; and the growth of the great and truthful features only of the national mind ensues. If, on the other hand, an established system were adopted, however judicious its arrangements might be – notwithstanding it might endeavour to promote liberality and independence of thought, it must eventually produce a general one-sidedness and similarity of character; and inasmuch as it did this, it would dry up the grand source of that spirit of agitation and inquiry, so essential as a stimulus to the improvement of the moral and intellectual man. (Spencer 1843, p. 231)

In the subsequent letter, Spencer explicitly compared the case for a national education, with the established church. For if national education is

to be truly a national one, it must be managed by the government, and sustained by state funds; those funds must form part of the revenue; that revenue is raised by taxation; that taxation falls upon every individual – upon him that has no children as well as upon him that has; and the result must be that all would pay towards the maintenance of such an institution, whether they had need of it or not – whether they approved of it or otherwise. (Spencer 1843, p. 228)

Opinions vary greatly, and it is impossible that everyone who will foot its bill will remain happy with the teaching supplied in state schools. Therefore,

> every argument used by religious nonconformists to show the unfairness of calling upon them to uphold doctrines that they cannot countenance, or subscribe towards a ministration which they do not attend, is equally effective in proving the injustice of compelling men to assist in the maintenance of a plan of instruction inconsistent with their principles; and forcing them to pay for teaching, from which neither they nor their children derive any benefit. In the one case, the spread of religious knowledge is the object aimed at – in the other the spread of secular knowledge. (Spencer 1843, pp. 240–1)

If both the government monopoly on education and the establishment of the Church of England are built on the idea that the state should 'look after the spiritual welfare of the community,' Spencer likewise rejected the idea there was a positive role for the public sector in promoting the physical welfare of people. It is indeed remarkable that, in 1842, well before anything like the Beveridge plan had crossed the mind of a politician, Spencer could see that 'the doctrine that it is the duty of the state to protect the public health, contains the germ of another gigantic monopoly.'

Spencer was specifically fighting against 'medical men endeavouring to establish a monopoly' in the form of restricting the supply of drug makers – as many of the latter exploit people's credulity. In a way, relying on a guild system in this way was the equivalent of what nowadays we may achieve by resorting to organizations such as the Food and Drug Administration (Spencer 1843, p. 245).

It is interesting to note the grounds on which Spencer opposed such a trend – because they entail an understanding of a mechanism not dissimilar from that of natural evolution. He wrote:

A large class of officiously humane people can never see any
social evil, but they propose to pass some law for its future
prevention. It never strikes them that the misfortunes of one
are lessons for thousands – that the world generally learns
more by its mistakes than by its successes – and that it is by
the continual endeavour to avoid errors, difficulties and dan-
gers, that society is to become wiser. It is not for a moment
denied that many individuals have been injured by druggists'
prescriptions, and quack medicines – some temporarily weakened – others permanently debilitated – and a few perhaps
killed outright. But, admitting this, it does not follow that it is
not the wisest in the end, to let things take their own course.
(Spencer 1843, p. 249)

'Nature provides nothing in vain.' For the performance of
any operation, 'every creature has its appropriate organs and
instincts – external apparatus and internal faculties; and the
health and happiness of each being are bound up with the per-
fection and activity of these powers.' Likewise, 'people are
naturally fitted to do for themselves.' They thrive, they adapt,
they make attempts, they make mistakes, but insuring people
against their mistakes cannot but create artificial obstacles to the
course of progress.[11]
     The tenth and eleventh letters are devoted to restating more
generally the case for small government. In the tenth letter
Spencer paradoxically claims that semi-free institutions – such
as the English ones, in his time – may provide a bad advertise-
ment for freedom. Even the subjects of oriental despotism can
point at many cases in England where not freedom but creeping
tyranny is endured. They are all the result of 'permitting our
rulers to spend their time and our money in the management
of matters over which they ought to have no control' which
will produce not only 'the evils arising from their mischievous
legislation, but likewise those resulting from the neglect of their
real duties' (Spencer 1843, pp. 255–6).

The eleventh letter takes instead the case of the enlargement of the franchise to the benefit of the working classes. The subject is crucial because, as we shall see later, Spencer developed a deep distrust of democracy as being ultimately inconsistent with individual freedom. But at the time these letters were written and printed, enfranchisement was advocated exactly by those very people who fought for the abolition of the Corn Laws, as well as for the repeal of the Poor Law.

Spencer reacts to the paternalist argument against enfranchisement ('Would it then, be prudent, to give to the uneducated classes, the power of directing the legislature in matters so difficult to understand, yet so important to the public welfare?') by emphasizing how those that oppose enfranchisement consider the duties of government too much. Allowing uneducated people to vote may be unwise only insofar as government is extending its reach in society so much that it could actually hinder its development. Complex and inappropriate legislation is the problem, not the franchise per se:

> If, then, it be admitted that our national misfortunes have not arisen from the difficulties inherent in the nature of government, but from the determination to legislate when no legislation was required – that is, if it be admitted that the administration of justice, is the sole duty of the state, we are at once relieved from one of the greatest objections to the enfranchisement of the working classes. (Spencer 1843, p. 259)

The Proper Sphere of Government is by no means the most original work by Spencer, but – as far as his politics is concerned – it is one of the most important. His later works in life tended to deal with the very same topics he touched upon in this very first work – sometimes reaching analogous positions, sometimes refining the argument, never rejecting the fundamental adhesion to the principles of individual liberty and limited government.

The Law of Equal Freedom and
the Principle of Utility

In *The Proper Sphere of Government*, the core of Spencer's political ideas is already crafted in the shape of a political program. These letters show a remarkable clarity of thought, but they are far from being the systematic articulation of a political theory. A 'system' is what Spencer tried to build all his life, and – before he started developing his *Synthetic Philosophy* (whose first bricks were the *Principles of Philosophy*) – *Social Statics* was the first attempt in that direction.

Published nine years after *The Proper Sphere of Government*, *Social Statics* was a far more ambitious undertaking. In this work, Spencer explained and reinforced his positions on topics such as the Poor Law, the regulation of commerce, healthcare policy and national education, but first and foremost his goal was 'to unfold that condition into a system of equity' (Spencer 1995, p. 66) – that is, the general principles of *Social Statics*. The subtitle is somewhat revealing: 'The Conditions Essential to Human Happiness and the First of Them Developed.' The book was intended as a correction of utilitarian philosophy, and as a restatement of the principles of classical liberalism in a tradition that was based on some version of the theory of natural rights, or better to say on 'moral sense.' Spencer could be interpreted as subscribing to a 'peculiar view of natural rights,' as stated by Leoni (2008, p. 99).

Entire libraries have been written on the relationship between Spencer and utilitarianism, but the question isn't settled yet. Spencer was commonly considered an 'anti-utilitarian' (among others, by John Stuart Mill),[12] but he never regarded himself as such (Spencer 1904, II, p. 88). On the contrary, he considered himself a 'rational utilitarian,' as opposed to the empirical ones. John Gray viewed 'Spencer's political thought as resting on a sort of indirect utilitarianism' (Gray 1982, p. 481). Weinstein sees Spencer as a '*self-consciously* utilitarian [who] makes a compelling case for rights-oriented, indirect utilitarianism.' This means

that he agreed on happiness as the fundamental human goal
but believed that

> utilitarians must adopt an indirect strategy because happiness
> is best maximized when all individuals develop their moral,
> mental and physical capacities by 'exercising' them . . . The
> only way to improve them is by *deciding for ourselves* as we strug-
> gle to resolve the moral and intellectual dilemmas we face.
> (Weinstein 1998, p.104)

Further,

> While preserving well-being as the ultimate ethical index,
> Spencer insisted that a true understanding of the laws of
> natural causation, as manifest in human society, made it clear
> that only if the state eschewed direct attempts to promote
> welfare and confined its function to safeguarding individual
> (negative claim) rights could present and future welfare actu-
> ally be maximized. (Meadowcroft 1995, p. 88)

In short, such a reformulation of utilitarianism nevertheless
served to place a primacy on the promotion of liberty over the
promotion of happiness.

That *Social Statics* is written *against* Benthamism is made apparent by its very author.[13] For Spencer, the most famous formulation of utilitarianism, the search for 'the greatest happiness for
all,' reveals that what he calls the expediency philosophy does
pursue 'the benefit of the mass, not the individual.' But even
more revealing is the fact that Spencer identifies the original sin
of utilitarianism in the fact it 'selects acts of Parliament for its
material, and employs the statesman for its architect' (Spencer
1995, p. 15). For utilitarians, 'the legislator is the great dispenser
of pleasures and pains in society' (Halevy 1966, p. 487). Utilitarianism 'takes government into partnership, assigns to it entire
control of its affairs, enjoins all to defer to its judgment – makes
it, in short, the vital principle, the very soul of its system' (Spencer
1995, p. 15). It is not so surprising, then, that a vehement

opponent of utilitarianism such as Murray N. Rothbard (1926–95) came to define *Social Statics as* 'the greatest single work of libertarian political philosophy ever written' (Rothbard 1971b, p. 5).[14]

For Spencer, claiming to be pursuing the greatest happiness for all meant that a political class was to assume it knew better what true happiness was for any individual citizen, and could therefore meddle with social engineering. But this would 'require nothing less than omniscience to carry it into practice' (Spencer 1995, p. 16). Spencer argues that 'no fact is more palpable than that the standard of happiness is infinitely variable' (Spencer 1995, p. 3) and scorns the legislators' futile attempt to do justice to the old utilitarian formula.

On the contrary, Spencer thought that (a) a system of morality should be centered on the individual, understanding from the outset that the state is a necessary evil, whose powers and obligations should be measured against the standard provided by any single individual, and (b) a system of morality should allow for the development (evolution was not the word yet) of mankind, providing different ethical standards according to the different stages of development:

> A system of moral philosophy professes to be a code of correct rules for the control of human beings . . . applicable, if true, to the guidance of humanity in its highest conceivable perfection. Government, however, is an institution originating in man's imperfection; an institution confessedly begotten by necessity out of evil . . . in short, inconsistent with the same 'highest conceivable perfection.' How, then, can that be a true system of morality which adopts government as one of its premises? (Spencer 1995, p. 16)

The original sin of Benthamites lay in the fact that they were somehow *compromised* with the state.

Gray aptly remarked that Spencer's moral theory is a 'doctrine of the individual moral sense in the form of a conclusion from methodological individualism' (Gray 1996, p. 20). The individual is the centre of Spencer's work. Spencer clearly states that 'there is no way of coming at a true theory of society but by inquiring into the nature of its component individuals. To understand humanity in its combinations, it is necessary to analyse that humanity in its elementary form' (Spencer 1995, p. 17). He did not reject the hedonistic principle of utilitarianism, but he reworked it in a way consistent with 'human behaviour as the laws of nature tell us it should be' (see Miller 1982, pp. 180–3).

Moral sense was adopted as the compass of Spencer's theory: 'We possess a "moral sense", the duty of which is to dictate rectitude in our transactions with each other, which receives gratification from honest and fair dealing, and which gives birth to the sentiment of justice' (Spencer 1995, p. 20). The moral sense is thus an *individual* quality, but it relates with *interpersonal dealings*; it guides the individual in having just relationships with other human beings. In his *Autobiography*, Spencer attempted to reconcile utilitarianism and moral sense by considering 'moral intuitions' as 'the results of accumulated experiences of utility, gradually organised and inherited' resulting in 'certain emotions responding to right and wrong conduct, which have no apparent basis on the individual experiences of utility' (Spencer 1904, II, p. 89). In other words, moral conscience was the product of the experiences of pleasure and pain of generations past.

In *Social Statics*, Spencer searched for moral sense in history, and he found it in all the different offspring of liberty from the Magna Carta to the Anti-Corn Law League. 'None but those committed to a preconceived theory can fail to recognize, on every hand, the workings of such a faculty.' 'Serfdom was abolished partly as its suggestion,' and it was moral sense that 'dictated Milton's *Essay on the Liberty of Unlicensed Printing*, that 'piloted the Pilgrim Fathers to the New World,' that 'through the mouths of anti-slavery orators, it poured out its fire to the scorching of the selfish, to the melting of the good, to our national purification.' It 'builds monuments to political martyrs, agitates for the admission of the Jews into Parliaments, publishes books on the rights of women, petitions against class legislation, threatens to rebel against militia conscription' (Spencer 1995, pp. 23–4).

Peel pointed out that *Social Statics* is the only book of Spencer's which is 'avowedly deist. Greatest happiness is "the Divine Idea", the exercise of faculties is "God's will and man's duty", man has "Divine authority" for claiming freedom' (Peel 1971, p. 83). In spite of his criticism of utilitarianism, Spencer upholds that 'it is one thing . . . to hold that greatest happiness is the creative purpose, and a quite different thing to hold that greatest happiness should be the *immediate* aim of man' (Spencer 1995, p. 61). Men should adopt to conditions conducive to happiness, as 'the doctrine is taught by all our religious teachers; it is assumed by every writer on morality; we may therefore safely consider it as an admitted truth.'

For Peel, Spencer was not 'fully aware of how much he assumed the moral residue of evangelicanism,' but somehow he understood that 'positive theism and teleological conceptions' were involved in *Social Statics*. Spencer thought that

> the supernaturalism was almost hidden behind the naturalism. Everything was referred to the unvarying course of causation, no less uniform in the spheres of life and mind than in the sphere of inanimate existence. Continuous adaptation was insisted on as holding of all organisms. (Spencer 1904, II, p. 7)

In subsequent works, 'divine will no longer served to anchor a moral theory but Spencer developed the doctrine of the "Unknowable".'[15]

It is true that *Social Statics* presents in a nutshell some of the claims that Spencer held dear throughout his life. It assumes a universal mutation of things and the world; it sees variability as inscribed in the laws of nature; and it forecasts progress in the continuous accumulation of knowledge and experience. Human beings are seen as evolving themselves, and their morality changes with circumstances as well. Foremost, Spencer already assumed that 'all evil results from the non-adaptation of constitution to conditions;' he saw life as requiring constant adaptation.[16] We can see here a fundamental idea of his system: that the cumulative effects of changes in nature amount to a process of evolution that constantly tends towards a state of equilibrium. Every living being exhibits a 'moving equilibrium – a system of mutually-dependent parts severally performing actions subserving maintenance of the combination' (Spencer 1904 II, p. 100). Adaptation emerges as a key concept in Spencer's ethics: he predicts the eventual attainment of a complete human adaptation to the social state, which is bound to be accompanied by a perfect social code.

As Spencer himself explained in writing the review of his own work he would have loved to have read, he

> considers Man as an organized being subject to the laws of life at large, and considers him as forced by increase of numbers into a social state which necessitates certain limitations to the actions by which he carries on life; and a cardinal doctrine, much emphasized by Mr Spencer, is that Man has been, and is, undergoing modifications of nature which fit him to the social state, by making conformity to these conditions spontaneous. (Spencer 1904, I, pp. 360–1)

In this process of evolution, Spencer distinguished between 'relative' and 'absolute' ethics, maintaining that what was morally right for a perfectly evolved humanity was not necessarily correct when such a perfect stage of evolution wasn't reached yet. As Miller (1982) emphasizes, the very title, *Social Statics*, explains that Spencer considered the study of society as a whole divided in between statics and dynamics. Most of the book is devoted to the equilibrium of a perfect (i.e. perfectly evolved) society, the rest to the 'dynamics' of transition. 'Failure to keep the nature of *Social Statics* in mind has been a major source of confusion about the development of Spencer's thought' (Miller 1982, p. 484). In other words, what was ethically correct for a perfectly evolved humanity was not necessarily so when the distorted facts of 'partially civilized' human natures were to be taken into

account. Perfect ethics could be taken as a benchmark: it being
a standard, 'relative justice has to be determined by considering
how near an approach may, under present circumstance, be
made to it' (Spencer 1978, I, p. 286). The value of absolute ethics is that we can use it to assess current moral conceptions.[17]

The cornerstone of Spencer's ethical theory is to be found in
what Spencer himself called 'the law of equal freedom,' which
is his fundamental principle of justice. The ultimate goal of an
individual, 'happiness,' (on that point, Spencer never abandoned the hedonistic view) is understood as depending on that
individual being in a position to exercise his own faculties: liberty comes in place as the necessary precondition for such an
exercise. Spencer derives it deductively from his own premises:
'God wills man's happiness. Man's happiness can be produced
only by the exercise of his faculties . . . But to exercise his faculties he must have liberty to do all that his faculties naturally
impel him to do. Then God intends he should have that liberty.
Therefore, he has a right to that liberty' (Spencer 1995, p. 69).

But since 'all must have rights to liberty of action . . . hence
there necessarily arises a limitation.' This limitation concerns
the possible clash of individuals pursuing mutually exclusive
ends:

> This sphere of existence into which we are thrown not afford-
> ing room for the unrestrained activity of all, and yet all pos-
> sessing in virtue of their constitutions similar claims to such
> unrestrained activity, there is no course but to apportion
> out the unavoidable restraint equally. Wherefore we arrive at
> the general proposition that every man may claim the fullest
> liberty to exercise his faculties compatible with the possession
> of like liberty by every other man. (Spencer 1995, p. 69)

As Spencer later explained in '*Justice*,'

> This formula has to unite a positive element with a negative
> element. It must be positive in so far as it asserts for each that,
> since he is to receive and suffer the good and evil results of his

actions, he must be allowed to act. And it must be negative in so far as, by asserting this of everyone, it implies that each can be allowed to act only under the restraint imposed by the presence of others having claim like this. (Spencer 1978, II, p. 61)

As Rothbard aptly remarked, Spencer's law of equal freedom 'does not attempt to make every individual's *total condition* equal – an absolutely impossible task; instead, but advocates liberty – a condition of absence of coercion over person and property for every man' (Rothbard 1970, p. 215).

'Freedom being the prerequisite to normal life in the individual, equal freedom becomes the prerequisite to normal life in society' (Spencer 1995, p. 79): for Spencer, the law of equal freedom ought to be the ultimate regulator of social life in a perfectly evolved society. But he actually used the law of equal freedom also as meter of judgement in his own time, perhaps because 'absolute ethics' (the ethics of the perfectly evolved society) was to also provide a standard for times of transition.

A very effective summary of the 'law of equal freedom' was supplied by Auberon Herbert, one of Spencer's most ardent disciples. Politics is

the science of determining the relations in which men can live together with the greatest happiness, and you will find that the axioms on which they depend are (1) that happiness consists in the exercise of faculties, (2) that as men have these faculties there must be freedom for their exercise, (3) that this freedom must be on equal and universal conditions, no unequal conditions satisfying out moral sense. (Herbert 1884, p. 97)

To prove Spencer's axioms, Herbert suggests to 'place before your mind the opposites of these statements, and try to construct a definite social system out of them.' Therefore 'happiness is not the exercise of faculties; men having faculties ought not to exercise them; the conditions as regard their exercise should be unequal and varying.' Then, Herbert asks, 'can you seriously maintain any of these statements?' (Herbert 1884, pp. 97–8).

On one hand, Spencer knew that 'justice imposes upon the exercise of faculties a primary series of limitations [and] negative beneficence imposes a secondary series' (Spencer 1995, p. 72). But as 'the limit put to each man's freedom, by the like freedom of every other man, is a limit almost always possible of exact ascertainment' (Spencer 1995, p. 73), questions of propriety or rules of conduct arising by the development of sympathy among men can never reach the status of certainty and, thus, applicability and legitimacy. Positive and negative beneficence play a role in Spencer's system besides stricter matters of justice.

On the other hand, Spencer knew that 'further qualifications of the liberty of action thus asserted may be necessary, yet . . . in the just regulation of community no further qualification of it can be recognized. Such further qualifications must ever remain for private and individual application' (Spencer 1995, p. 95). This means that individuals are in a position to mutually bind each other by consent and contract (see Barnett 1998, pp. 74–7).

In Spencer's system, the law of equal freedom gives rise to 'rights.' In *Social Statics* as well as in *'Justice,'* Spencer explains that 'rights, truly called, are the corollaries from the law of equal freedom' (Spencer 1978, II, p. 80) and not the product of legislative fiat. Such corollaries are enumerated in both works: from the right to physical integrity to the right to free motion, from the right of property, to the rights of free exchange and others – all of them being 'specifications' of the general principle of equal freedom, in different societal and economic realms. As is well known, the key difference in the enumeration of these rights in *Social Statics* and in *'Justice'* lies in the fact that Spencer partially changed his mind over 'the right to use the earth,' the rights of women and the right to vote. We will subsequently investigate these questions in some detail. Spencer did not come back to the 'the right to ignore the state' (the possibility to exit from a state community in a situation of voluntary citizenship)[18] – included in the 1851 edition of *Social Statics* but abridged from the reprints – and indeed he repudiated it.[19]

In Spencer's work, these rights, deriving from the law of equal freedom, are not just essential for individual life but also for the life of society. The proper fabric of social life can come to work only insofar as the different parts of societies are allowed to perform their functions and receive the necessary rewards for this activity.

These rights can be considered 'natural' and 'pre-political.' They come before the state, and are kept to a narrow and precise list. None of them can be read as an entitlement that an individual can claim from the state: they all imply a restraint on the part of other individuals or of the government, instead of entailing any positive action on their part.

Not surprisingly, then, the law of equal liberty and its corollaries led Spencer to limit the duties of the state to those typically envisioned by theorists of the minimal state: defence from foreign aggression and protection from aggression of other men.

Militancy and Industrialism

In *Social Statics,* as in the later body of his work, Spencer 'affirmed that human society evolves just as the human species has evolved' (Gray 1982, p. 468). *'Political Institutions'* (the fifth part of the *Principles of Sociology*) and *'Justice'* (the fourth part of the *Principles of Ethics*) are the principal works in which he clarified his view of societal progress. 'Progress' and 'evolution' are intertwined concepts: in charting the changes of human societies in history, Spencer projected a trajectory of future developments as well.

One of the key sources of evolution in human societies was the growth of population. Spencer thought that 'from the beginning, pressure of population has been the proximate cause of progress' (Spencer 1852). Population pressure forces men to be more effective, and social habits develop accordingly to make the best use of the surrounding environment. 'Differentiation, specialization, the division of labour, come about because they are more adaptive' (Peel 1971, p. 139).

Different conditions to which human societies should adapt produce a trend of evolution that goes necessarily from militancy to industrialism. This is the scene upon which his political theory is staged. As Meadowcroft noted, 'the concepts of "justice", "freedom" and "rights" are used throughout Spencer's works to circumscribe tightly the functions that legitimately can be assumed by the state as the industrial type is more closely approached' (Meadowcroft 1995, p. 77).

Militant societies are characterized by features that proved advantageous to the 'survival of the fittest' in the physical struggle for existence among societies. There is a tendency towards the growth of corporate structures that makes it possible to effectively mobilize resources for war. In its most developed form, a militant society displays a highly hierarchical and centralized decision-making system, a pervasive control of the activity of its individual members, and government action which is both 'positively' and 'negatively' regulative. In Spencer's view, positive regulation implies governmental acts that 'stimulate and direct,' whereas negative regulation connotes only restraint (Spencer 1871, p. 145). 'So long as militancy predominates, the constitution of the state must be one in which the ordinary citizen is subject either to an autocrat or to an oligarchy' (Spencer 1981, II, p. 210).

Positive regulation fits in the evolution of societies, insofar as they need to resist attack in an aggressive environment. The chain of command needs to be short, the army responsive, the social groups should stay coalesced. The militant society is 'a regime of status, since its members stand one towards another in successive grades of subordination. From the despot down to the slaves, all are masters of those below and subjects of those above' (Spencer 1882, p. 663).

In the industrial society, on the other hand, the needs to be satisfied are very different: decision-making is better kept decentralized, as more conducive to social welfare, and hierarchy is confined to the remnants of the militant type, namely within the government and the army. To win a war, you need plans, strategy and a strict implementation of orders. For the peaceful conduct of business, the implementation of contracts and protections against aggression are necessary.

Underpinning this dichotomy between military and industrial society, there is a distinction between coercive and voluntary forms of social cooperation. Everywhere, the 'organization evolved for governmental and defensive purposes' was the output of efforts to promote public ends via compulsion, whereas the 'organization shown us by the division of labour for industrial purposes' emerged spontaneously from the individuals' efforts to promote their welfare and was built on voluntary cooperation (Spencer 1882, p. 247).

Men originally came together for three reasons: the first is the 'desire of companionship,' the second is 'the need for combined action against enemies' and the third is 'facilitating sustentation by mutual aid.' Spencer highlights how the first aim leads to 'aggregation,' whereas the second and the third produce 'cooperation' – as we already saw, typically compulsory cooperation (for warlike efforts) and voluntary cooperation (for better satisfying each and everybody's needs via market exchange).

If the division of labour is a typical trait of humankind, the way in which it is implemented constitutes the key difference between militancy and industrialism. The struggle for existence between tribes engendered the emergence of the military type. Warfare motivated the very first form of specialization within a tribe, with a permanent chieftain and a warrior elite establishing a system of hierarchy. The creation of social classes is a by-product of this process. In Turner's words, for Spencer, 'those with power use it to create and sustain privilege, which in turn generates tensions between those with and without resources. Such production of classes is a direct function of the concentration of political power' (Turner 1985, p. 126).

Militancy creates political inequalities but increasing industrialism rebuffs them. 'This acts in two ways – firstly, by creating a class having power derived otherwise than from territorial possessions or official positions; and, secondly, by generating ideas and sentiments at variance with the ancient assumptions of class-superiority.' Any and each type of society is sustained by different sentiments and encourages different virtues. Whereas in a military state the individual is understood as a unit disposable on behalf of the whole of society, in the industrial society all social agreements are voluntarily chosen and men are only considered as belonging to the associations (or clubs) they voluntarily enroll in. The notion of sacrificing the single individual for the sake of society flourishes in the one context, whereas privacy and individuality are socially rewarded in the other.

Somehow, however, militancy was preparing the ground for the emergence of industrialism. Military societies helped in *integrating* human beings into larger aggregates: 'With this advance from small incoherent social aggregates to great coherent ones, which, while becoming integrated pass from uniformity to multiformity, there goes an advance from indefiniteness of political organization to definiteness of political organization' (Spencer 1882, p. 252). Only insofar as this process of integration is sufficiently advanced, the process of *differentiation* that leads to industrialism can take off.

> It is only after conquest has consolidated small communities into larger ones, that arise opportunities for the growth of mutual dependence among men who have devoted themselves to different industries. Hence throughout long periods the industrial organization, merely subservient to the militant organization, has had its essential nature disguised. (Spencer 1978, II, p. 205)

Militancy also helps to set the stage for industrialism by encouraging 'the power of continuous application, the willingness to act under direction (now no longer coercive but agreed to under contract) and the habit of achieving large results by organizations' (Spencer 1981, p. 186).

The industrial type of society was for Spencer the ultimate social output of evolution, as he conceived it. In society, as in nature, 'Progress is not an accident, not a thing within human control, but a beneficent necessity' (Spencer 1857, p. 195). The industrial type was a society more 'developed' and more 'individualized,' where an evermore complex division of labour brought by an increasing differentiation between individuals.[20] Uniformity declined, pluralism sprang up.

The ideal of industrialism is a regime in which 'the citizen's individuality, instead of being sacrificed by the society, has to be defended by the society. Defence of his individuality becomes the society's essential duty' (Spencer 1882, p. 539). Industrial societies are adapted for peace: they present a decentralized and representative system of government, self-directed economic activities on the part of the individual members, a merely 'negatively regulative' kind of action on the part of their governments. In the industrial model, 'for the society having as an aggregate no sentiency, its preservation is a desideratum only as subserving individual sentiencies. How does it subserve individual sentiencies? Primarily by preventing interferences with the carrying on of individual lives' (Spencer 1978, II, p. 206). The social order of an industrial society is a 'spontaneous order' – to use a familiar formula – and this implies that the 'spontaneously formed social organization is so bound together that you cannot act on one part without acting more or less on all parts' (Spencer 1981, p. 135). An industrial society is in essence 'a purified form of the market society which had developed in nineteenth-century England, with various remnants of earlier ("militant") society removed' (Miller 1976, p. 185).

The contrast between 'warriors' (the leading characters of the militant type) and 'merchants' (the champions of the industrial one) is so crucial, in Spencer's analysis, that he also thought that political parties are seen to arise directly or indirectly out of the conflict between militancy and industrialism. Either they stand respectively for the coercive government of the one and the free government of the other, or for particular institutions and laws belonging to the one or the other. (Spencer 1882, p. 157)

Spencer read history as displaying a general movement from militancy to industrialism.[21] It should be clarified that these generalizations are not purely theoretical. As anthropologist Robert Carneiro observed, Spencer's pioneering sociological work 'contained many generalizations, functional and evolutionary, suggested or supported by a wealth of ethnographic and historical facts. It carried sociology and anthropology far beyond where it had stood before' (Carneiro 1981, p. 167).

The evolution from the militant type to the industrial type can be read also as the evolution from *status* to *contract*, to use Henry Maine's terminology. Sir Henry Maine's chief concern was *legal* progress, which he understood as being somehow the fruit of progress in society all together. For Maine, law did not produce, but rather, reacted to social change: law binds society together, but 'social necessities and social opinion are always more or less in advance of Law' (Maine 1905, p. 24).

The words '*status*' and '*contract*' are explicitly used in *Ancient Law* and forcefully linked as the beginning and the end of the civilization process. 'The movement of progressive societies has been uniform in one respect. Through all its course it has been distinguished by the gradual dissolution of family dependency, and the growth of individual obligation in its place' (Maine 1905, p. 168). 'The movement of the progressive societies has hitherto been a movement *from Status to Contract.*' Ancient times, Maine noted, knew nothing like the individual

[which is] one peculiarity invariably distinguishing the infancy of society. Men are regarded and treated not as individuals, but always as members of a particular group. Everybody is first a citizen, and then, as a citizen, he is a member of his order . . . next, he is a member of a gens, house of clan . . . His individuality was swallowed up in his family. (Maine 1905, p. 183)

For Maine, progress comes together with differentiation, i.e. with the true emergence of individuality. History of law is then to be examined carefully to understand 'by what insensible gradations the relation of man to man substituted itself for the relations of the individual to his family, and of families to each other' (Maine 1905, p. 224).

Status and contract are the juridical counterparts of militancy and industrialism: they occupy two opposite poles in evolution.

There are few general propositions concerning the age to which we belong which seem at first sight likely to be received with readier concurrence than the assertion that the society of our day is mainly distinguished from that of preceding generations by the largeness of the sphere which is occupied in it by Contract. Some of the phenomena on which this proposition rests are among those most frequently singled out for notice, for comment, and for eulogy. Not many are so unobservant as not to perceive that in innumerable cases where old law fixed a man's social position irreversibly at his birth, modern law allows him to create it for himself by convention: and indeed several of the few exceptions which remain to this rule are constantly denounced with passionate indignation. (Maine 1905, p. 304)

The view that liberty-oriented societies were relatively new in history, and profoundly different from previous political regimes, is by no means exclusive to Spencer and Maine. It is, in a way, one of the fundamental themes of the classical liberal tradition.

In these circumstances, the name of Benjamin Constant (1767–1830) immediately comes to mind. For Constant,

[the] social organization [of the ancient] led them to desire an entirely different freedom from the one which this system grants to us . . . Among the ancients the individual, almost always sovereign in public affairs, was a slave in all his private relations. As a citizen, he decided on peace and war; as a private individual, he was constrained, watched and repressed in all his movements; as a member of the collective body, he interrogated, dismissed, condemned, beggared, exiled, or sentenced to death his magistrates and superiors; as a subject of the collective body he could himself be deprived of his status, stripped of his privileges, banished, put to death, by the discretionary will of the whole to which he belonged. (Constant 1819, p. 310)

Liberty in modern times is *individual*, it is connected to the development of *abstract*, contract relations – as opposed to face-to-face relations in ancient society.

In a similar vein, Spencer maintained that

the time was when the history of a people was but the history of its government. It is otherwise now. The once universal despotism was but a manifestation of the extreme necessity of restraint. Feudalism, serfdom, slavery – all tyrannical institutions – are merely the most vigorous kinds of rule, springing out, and necessary to, a bad state of man. The progress from these is in all cases the same – less government. (Spencer 1995, p. 14)

Industrialism and Pacifism

From *the Proper Sphere of Government* on, Spencer was a full-fledged pacifist. Opposition to imperialism and war is nowadays typically associated with left-leaning political doctrines that see in the imperial rule of industrial Western states some sort of 'externalization' of the process of exploitation which is the black heart of the capitalism system.

This was not always the case. Opposition to the imperial dreams of the British ruling class was one of the distinctive traits of classical liberalism: Edmund Burke opposed initiatives to curb the rebellion of the American colonies; Richard Cobden campaigned extensively for peace; and Herbert Spencer was moved by the topic of aggressive wars more than anything else.[22]

Like Cobdenites, Spencer condemned war for the destruction it caused, both on social and economic grounds. As he highlighted in the *Proper Sphere of Government*, war was not by chance the single cause of England's public debt. War deprived individuals and families of their loved ones, and brought misery to society at large. For Spencer this was a crucial issue. He was deeply emotional on the subject; the only time in his life when he was tempted by the dubious lure of political action, was when he unsuccessfully tried – with John Bright and others – to constitute an Anti-Aggression League in 1881. He condemned the war in South Africa in 1899 and the Afghan War too. He commented that 'the white savages of Europe are overrunning the dark savages everywhere' and that they were entering 'an era of social cannibalism in which the strong nations are devouring the weaker' (Duncan 1908, II, p. 135).

Within his system, the British aggressive behaviour signalled also a resurgence of the pre-industrial spirit, a U-turn on the way to social evolution. For the very same reason, he feared the emergence of political doctrines supportive of the imperial efforts – as both militancy and industrialism, Spencer knew, were characterized not only by institutions but also by different supporting ideas widespread in the public opinion.

One of the articles included in *Facts and Comments*, tells a revealing story:

Some years ago I gave my expression to my own feeling – anti-patriotic feeling, it will doubtless be called – in a somewhat startling way. It was at the time of the second Afghan war, when, in pursuance of what were thought to be 'our interests,' we were invading Afghanistan. News had come that some of our troops were in danger. At the Athenæum Club a well-known military man – then a captain but now a general – drew my attention to a telegram containing this news, and read it to me in a manner implying the belief that I should share his anxiety. I astounded him by replying, 'When men hire themselves out to shoot other men to order, asking nothing about the justice of their cause, I don't care if they are shot themselves.'

For Spencer,

the cry, 'Our country, right or wrong!' seems detestable. By association with love of country the sentiment it expresses gains a certain justification. Do but pull off the cloak, however, and the contained sentiment is seen to be of the lowest. Let us observe the alternative cases. Suppose our country is in the right – suppose it is resisting invasion. Then the idea and feeling embodied in the cry are righteous. It may be effectively contended that self-defence is not only justified but is a duty. Now suppose, contrariwise, that our country is the aggressor – has taken possession of others' territory, or is forcing by arms certain commodities on a nation which does not want them, or is backing up some of its agents in 'punishing' those who have retaliated. Suppose it is doing something which, by the hypothesis, is admitted to be wrong. What is then the implication of the cry? The right is on the side of those who oppose us; the wrong is on our side. (Spencer 1902, pp. 124–5)

Such a committed opposition to militarism wasn't just a *cri de coeur*. Warfare was the fundamental cause of militancy, and the perils of its resurgence laid exactly there.

In modern times, war is indeed the health of the state. One of the most characteristic functions of the modern state, notes

Martin van Creveld, has been 'to wage war against others of
its kind.'

> Had it not been for the need to wage war against others of its
> kind; had it not been for the need to wage war, then almost
> certainly the centralization of power in the hands of the great
> monarchs would have been much harder to bring about. Had
> it not been for the need to wage war, then the development of
> bureaucracy, taxation, even welfare services such as education,
> health, etc., would probably have been much slower. As the
> record shows, in one way or another, all of them were origi-
> nally bound up with the desire to make people more willing
> to fight on behalf of their respective states. (Van Creveld 1999,
> p. 336)

Spencer did see liberty at home and non-aggressive foreign
policy as fundamentally tied: he understood them to as the two
sides of industrialism's coin. Political progress should have gone
hand-in-hand with a reduction of armed conflicts among states.
International peace would 'greatly check aggressive behaviour
towards one another; and, by doing this, would diminish the
coerciveness of their governmental systems while appropriately
changing their political theories' (Spencer 1981, p. 92).

In a way, the theory of the *doux commerce* is an integral part
of Spencer's system. In social evolution, women and men move
from compulsory division of labour to voluntary division of
labour. This process is a move from hierarchies to markets, but
first and foremost, from coercive cooperation to free cooperation. This change entails the development of relationships
framed in freedom, which makes for civilization and for the
development of altruism.

The spread of commerce implies not only peaceful relations
among countries, but the growth of industrialism and the
enlargement of the sphere of freedom at home. A market society is thus more peaceful and even *kinder* by the very fact that
status becomes less important in determining the fundamental

social relationships, and people are at liberty to make up their social world and to establish fruitful and pleasant and fully voluntary relationships with other human beings. The development of technology, with ever-increasing power for virtually any individual to create her own social world, to develop friendships and acquaintances regardless of physical distances – and therefore to be ever less dependent on the mere chance of having been born here or there – adds up to this process that writers such as Constant and Spencer were able to anticipate in its fundamentals some two hundred years ago.

The 'civilizing effect' of market arrangements is far from being undisputed. John Meadowcroft has perceptively noted that 'many critiques of the social impact of the market appear to view the market as a distinct entity from civil society' (Meadowcroft 2005, p. 147). Socialists (who argue capitalism 'alienates' large portions of the population) and communitarians (*laudatores temporis actii*, who would like individuals to be more firmly rooted in their social settings) have profoundly questioned this view. Thomas Carlyle (1795–1881) was one of Spencer's most famous contemporaries, and he argued forcefully that the law of supply and demand, rooted in the dismal science of economics, was bound to engender social disruption. Many writers, within the socialist and the conservative traditions alike, ended up, on the contrary, depicting capitalism as a force destroying all pre-existing social institutions, including the traditional and religious sources of morality and, particularly, the institution of family and marriage. An enlargement of the sphere of the free market spreads 'commodification' in society, and thus trashes established moral values.

Spencer belonged to quite a different tradition of thought. As Gertrude Himmelfarb noted, even for Adam Smith 'industrialism and commerce were not only the instruments for material improvement . . . They were also the means by which the men could exercise their desire for "betterment"' (Himmelfarb 2004, pp. 65–6). Spencer would agree, as he would concur with economist Deidre McCloskey who, in a recent work, building on the

Smithian tradition of thought, asserted that 'participation in capitalist markets and bourgeois virtues has civilized the world' (McCloskey 2006, p. 26).

The Fate of the Unfit

As we saw, Spencer had opposed the Poor Law ever since the publication of *The Proper Sphere of Government*. For one thing, making the state a machine serving the goal of income redistribution was 'improper' as far as justice was concerned: it implied an expansion of the scope and the duties of the state which was inconsistent with the strict limitations advocated by Spencer. For another, the Poor Law was ultimately adding a burden on the working classes: it punished the working poor to reward the idle. In fact, the issue of poverty – and the concern with the 'deserving' vis-à-vis the 'undeserving' poor – was a quintessentially Victorian trait (see Himmelfarb 1992).

The label of social Darwinist that sticks to Spencer's name up to our times, reveals a common suspicion that he was 'insensitive' to the plight of the poor. In this respect, Spencer shares the fate of many other advocates of the market system who are understood to prize allocative efficiency over any other social goal.

This is best epitomized by what is probably the most renowned Adam Smith quotation: 'It is not from the benevolence of the butcher, the brewer or the baker that we expect our dinner, but from their regard to their own interest' (Smith 1937, p. 14) This principle was based on the assumption that the butcher, brewer and baker operated in what Smith called the 'system of natural liberty,' that is, a market-based society that allowed for the exchange of goods and services without the interference of the state, to the benefit of all the partners in the exchange. For Smith, it was instead the mercantilist system – directing and guiding the economy for the sake of national power – that encouraged men to aggressive and egoist behavior. In The *Wealth of Nations*, Smith observed that in a civilized society 'man has almost constant occasion for the help of his brethren.'

The system of natural liberty (and not state intervention) made self-interest conducive to the general interest. The metaphor of the invisible hand was an efficacious illustration of how the good of society was advanced by the unintended consequences of individual (and self-interested) actions. Without outside intervention and (perhaps even more importantly) without any conscious complete understanding of the effects of his own action, each individual is 'led by an invisible hand to promote an end which was no part of his intention' (Smith 1937, p. 423).

Gertrude Himmelfarb recently remarked that

> Smith's opposition to mercantilism is generally read as a criticism of government regulation and a defense of a policy of laissez-faire. It was that, and much more as well. Mercantilism not only inhibited a progressive economy by interfering with the natural processes of the market. It was also, Smith charged, unjustly biased against workers because it set maximum rather than minimum wages, thus benefiting merchants and manufacturers at the expense of the workers . . . A free market, Smith argued, combined with the division of labour would permit the economy to expand, absorbing the higher wages and increased population, and bringing with it not misery and vice for the common man but a 'plentiful subsistence' and the comfortable hope of 'bettering his conditions.' (Himmelfarb 2004, pp. 60, 62)

Already in *Social Statics*, Spencer wanted to go beyond a 'purely selfish . . . instinct of personal rights . . . leading each man to assert and defend his own liberty of action.' The concept of sympathy that Spencer borrowed from Adam Smith to show how 'justice and beneficence have a common root . . . sympathy' (Spencer 1995, pp. 89, 91) comes in handy here. McCann wrote that 'treatment of moral obligation may best be seen as an extension of Adam Smith's presentation in *Theory of Moral Sentiments*' (McCann 2004, p. 97). Spencer was himself acquainted with *The Theory of Moral Sentiments* and he acknowledged that "the doctrine of sympathy had already been set forth by him [Adam Smith]; but it would seem that having reached it in the endeavour to explain benevolence, I subsequently carried it on to explain justice" (Spencer 1904, I, p. 229).

In The *Principles of Ethics*, Spencer considered the positive obligations for the individual as far as concerned the relief of the poor – and insisted that they were real – drawing a line between 'justice' and 'benevolence.'

Two principles present in 'animal ethics' – that is, in the moral ordainment of the animal worlds – were crucial for Spencer:

> First, that among adults there must be conformity with the law that benefits received shall be divided proportionate to merits possessed: merits being measured by power of self-sustentation . . . Second, that during early life, before self-sustentation has become possible, and also while it can be but partial, the aid must be the greatest where the worth shown is the smallest – benefits received must be inversely proportionate to merits possessed: merits being measured by the power of self-sustentation. (Spencer 1978, I, p. 22)

The first principle informed what Spencer considered the 'law of conduct and consequence': equal freedom implied that each human being, free to pursue his own preferred course of action insofar as it did not cause damage to his fellow man, should bear the consequences of his conduct.

As David Miller clarified, 'Spencer identifies justice with a distribution according to desert, desert here being interpreted as "achievement" and not as "effort"' (Miller 1976, p. 186). Moreover, 'Each individual shall receive the benefits and the evils of its own consequent conduct' (Spencer 1978, II, p. 17). The idea of a distribution according to desert *implies* inequalities in distribution. In a way, the law of equal freedom needed, so to say, a 'law of equal responsibility' clearly linking retributions and conducts.

This is a form of 'survival of the fittest' that imbued the history of humankind: but in industrial society, this was not the survival

of the physically stronger but rather 'the survival of the industri-
ally superior and those who are fittest for requirements of social
life' (Spencer 1885, p. 127). In industrial societies, the struggle
for life doesn't cease but becomes *kinder*. The very process of
evolution demands that society puts 'a check upon that part
of the cosmic process which consists of unqualified struggle for
existence.'

In a sense, a society which is less and less warlike can clearly
endorse more compassionate behaviour. By the very substitution
of the sword with the contract-signing pen, human relations are
becoming more peaceful and understanding. But Spencer also
believed that, as we progress towards industrialism, there was
room for human solidarity.

Spencer distinguished 'justice' and 'beneficence,' avoiding
any confusion between the two (Spencer 1978, II, p. 294). Justice
had to do with the ordering of social relations: the law of equal
freedom concerned the legitimate way of interacting with one
another in society, and so in economical undertakings. But
he also believed that justice needed to be tempered by benevolence, especially private charity, which was not demanded by a
just ordering of society but by the development of sympathy.
The development of altruistic moral sentiments was an essential
factor in the evolution of humanity. He was also convinced that,
with the evolution of society and morals, the rich would be ever
'devoting more energy to furthering the material and mental
progress of the masses' (Spencer 1859, p. 150).

For Nisbet, 'despite common belief that the upshot of Spencer's
passion for freedom was merely giving licence to the rich and
powerful . . . there is a strong and persisting vein of humanitarian-
ism in his works' (Nisbet 1980, p. 232). As Tim S. Gray has noted,
'a considerable part of Spencer's ethical theory was devoted to the
justification of altruism as moral duty which frequently overrode
the egoistic "duty" to "self"' (Gray 1996, p. 28). Spencer himself
remarked, thinking of his critics, 'I do not see how there could be
ideas more diametrically opposed to that brutal individualism
which some persons ascribe to me' (Spencer 1898, p. 128).

Spencer distinguished between negative and positive beneficence: negative beneficence involved self-restraint, positive beneficence involved providing help and aid of the disadvantaged.
In actual fact, Spencer also deemed negative beneficence to be
likewise required in the conduct of business. In this respect
he can be said to be advocating a suboptimal level of conduct in
the economic world for the sake of making social arrangements
smoother. Positive beneficence was required for the higher
stages of evolution because they were actually possible only when
human beings were so constituted that 'each, in addition to the
pleasurable emotions received by him, can sympathetically participate in the pleasurable emotions of all others' (Spencer 1995,
p. 84).

Occasionally Spencer's concerns for the poorer layers of
society can be overlooked because of the lexicon he was employing, and because of his forceful opposition to the development
of state-provided poverty relief. Two points should be stressed.
The first one is that just as it is not necessary to advocate a government buyout of football teams to be a football fan, so it is
by no means necessary to argue for state involvement in charity
to be a humanitarian. The Victorian age saw the development
of many privately funded and managed 'safety net' systems, and
even today private charity continues to exist (supplied by individuals, religious or secular organizations, and private foundations), in spite of the 'crowding out' effects of ever-larger state
involvement in 'benevolence.' The second one is that the nineteenth century was the century of 'self help.' The distinction
between deserving and undeserving poor was crucial and widespread, not only within the boundaries of the individualist
movement. The fear that by helping individuals the state may
deprive them of the disposition to help themselves was common:
demoralizing the poor by aiding them was seen as a peril to
be avoided. Positive schemes for eradicating poverty were thus
looked upon with suspicion, as they undermined spontaneous
solidarity in society.

The Occasional Communist

In *Social Statics* Spencer proclaimed that 'equity . . . does not permit property in land' (Spencer 1995, p. 103). In his treatise, Spencer defended private property with the same strength he displayed in *The Proper Sphere of Government,* but made an exception for property in land. He departed from Lockean liberalism precisely on this question. On this point, he was heavily criticized by his friend Thomas Hodgskin in Hodgskin's review of *Social Statics* in *The Economist.*

As Halevy explains, for Hodgskin,

> this type of communism . . . involves the confusion of the right of the individual to the use of his faculties with his right to the use of the soil: it does not take account of the fact that, with the progress of the arts, an increasing number of individuals can work and receive the product of their labour without sharing in the possession of the soil; it withdraws from individuals the right of ownership to give that to societies, when societies have no other rights than the sum of the rights of the individuals. (Halevy 1956, p. 142)

Because of this crucial difference in thinking between the two friends, Stack is actually sceptical of Hodgkins' influence over Spencer: Hodgskin's chief influence was Locke, an author whom Spencer may have not even read. Spencer's position on land 'was repeating one of the central fallacies that Hodgskin had set out to demolish . . . Whereas Locke had understood the land being given in common, *res nullius,* and belonging to no one, Spencer wrote of the land belonging to mankind' (Stack 1998, p. 192). Francis goes as far as to write that 'the labour theory of value seemed absurd to Spencer: he could not comprehend why the extermination of a set of plants or the ploughing of the soil to the depth of a few inches proved a claim to the earth beneath' (Francis 2007, p. 254).

To be sure, Spencer cannot say how a valid claim could be shown on property in land. Property in land is supposed to be against the law of equal freedom precisely because property implies exclusivity, and since the earth is God's bequest to mankind, everyone should be allowed to make use of it in a way that does not prevent the others from doing so as well. This is certainly impossible in a regime of private property. In Hillel Steiner's synthesis, Spencer maintained that 'to have any right at all, an individual must have a right not only to his own body, but also to terrestrial space: people are not "floating wraiths"' (Steiner 1982, p. 527).

Going back all the way to the origin of property rights, he saw that, as far as land property was concerned, 'the original deeds were written with the sword rather than with the pen: not lawyers, but soldiers, were the conveyancers' (Spencer 1995, p. 104). He saw a link between 'militancy and landowning' (Spencer 1882, p. 46). Historically, he argued, land was redistributed by victorious military leaders to their best warriors and comrades. The property of land was therefore the quintessential mark of a 'warrior class,' an oligarchy that gained its status by the sword.

The idea that individuals peacefully acquired property rights in a pre-political state by mixing their labour with the goods provided by nature could not fit into the scheme of somebody envisioning the dynamics of society as a progress from militancy to industrialism. If private property in other goods is typically the result of personal thrift, of inventions, of creativity, private property in land – Spencer assumed – was by necessity to be grounded in conquest. In some respects this view is less consistent with Spencer's liberal progenitors than with what we may call the 'constituency' of his readers. The great enemy of liberals was the landed aristocracy, which was regarded as 'the section of society most hopelessly corrupted by unchecked power, excessive authority and influence, and the lack of exertion and daily labour' (Biagini 1992, p. 51).

Spencer, however, never enlisted in the ranks of violent expropriators. Though not a follower of Locke, in his work he compared the improvements added to land by mixing labour with it with the repairs made by a casual guest to an ostensibly deserted house. If the legitimate owner were to come back, the squatters should leave the house but are entitled 'to an equitable title to compensation from the proprietor for repairs and new fittings' (Spencer 1995, p. 108). In Spencer's scheme, land should be 'the joint ownership of the public,' with single 'occupants' reduced to *affictuaries* of society (Spencer 1995, p. 111). By leasing a tract of land from society, a person could mix her labour with the land and be entitled to the fruits of her toil: that is because she 'obtained the *consent* of society before so expanding' her labor (Spencer 1995, p. 116).

How the transition from a private property system to a communal system was to be managed is unclear. What is clear is that Spencer didn't feel any nostalgia for pre-modern society, where the soil was commonly managed; he didn't want the joint ownership of land to serve as a lever to abandon industrialism (as underlined by Steiner 1982, p. 528). At the end of the day, Spencer's position on land is in some way not dissimilar from the view held by contemporary so-called 'left-libertarianism.'[23] G. A. Cohen (1941–2009) considers Spencer to have been a 'left-libertarian' (i.e. in his view, a libertarian who is 'an egalitarian with respect to initial shares in external resources') in his youth before becoming 'a right-wing libertarian' (Cohen 1995, p. 118 and p. 118 n.). The idea that Spencer experienced a 'drift to conservatism' in later years is widespread, and largely built on his change of mind on land ownership.

On the issue of property, he certainly grew increasingly worried by the possibility that his 1851 work could be used as an argument supporting socialistic doctrines he otherwise opposed. In particular, Henry George (1839–97) alluded to the land doctrine of *Social Statics* in his *Progress and Poverty* (George 1879), to Spencer's dismay. Spencer refers in derogatory terms to George in *Man Versus the State*, expressing hostility to the 'communistic theory' embodied in 'the movement for land nationalization.'

Spencer marked his distance from George in a series of public statements (including a letter to *The Times*)[24] but came to restate his theory in '*Justice.*' There, he did not dismantle his theoretical edifice; as Paul has noted, 'Spencer's arguments for collective ownership of the land do not vary appreciably from *Social Statics* to 'Justice'" (Paul 1982, p. 509).

For one thing, he referred to his own distinction between relative and absolute ethics: *Social Statics* was chiefly concerned with the ethical arrangements that will be in place among perfectly morally evolved men, and not in the present transition age.[25] But it is far more interesting that Spencer came to devote more and more attention to the 'history' of the claims over land, and therefore to the problem of rectification of initial injustices. Before the enclosures movement, land property was largely regulated by a vast array of communal and allodial rights. Whenever land was property of a single family, this was a uniformly aristocratic one. He builds on the fact that the origins of particular claims are lost in the mists of history: 'the fact is that in early stages private ownership of land is unknown: only the usufruct belongs to the cultivator, while the land itself is tacitly regarded as the property of the tribe' (Spencer 1978, II, p. 102). He observes that 'conquest from without has everywhere been chiefly instrumental in superseding communal proprietorship by individual proprietorship' (Spencer 1978, II, p. 105) and by doing so he succeeds in grounding his views on property in his more general vision of history.

By stating the problem in these terms (the lack of legitimacy of titles of property which originated in conquest), Spencer needs to face the dilemmas of rectification. In an appendix to '*Justice,*' Spencer comes to oppose land nationalization because of its ultimate unfeasibility. His theory was built on the idea that current landowners could not exhibit a valid claim to land, but reconstructing history to determine who was the conqueror and who was the exploited is ultimately impossible:

> Even supposing that the English as a race gained possession of the land equitably, which they did not; and even supposing

that existing landowners are the posterity of those who spoiled their fellows, which in large part they are not; and even supposing that the existing landless are the posterity of the despoiled, which in large part they are not; there would still have to be recognized a transaction that goes far to prevent rectification of injustice. (Spencer 1981, II, p. 458)

Spencer did not change his mind on the source of ownership in land, but he acknowledged the role of exchanges and developments in history. He saw that most of the value of the land was due to efforts of different generations of landlords and 'cannot without a gigantic robbery be taken from them.'

Between *Social Statics* and The *Principles of Ethics*, Spencer developed his *sociology*, which is perhaps still his most lasting contribution to the world of social science. The new conclusion reached regarding the property of land is actually much more in line with Spencer's sociological thinking, which does not aim at social engineering, but rather claims to provide an understanding of society and its historical mutation.

Also, towards the end of his life he realized (quite consistently with the general outlook of his thinking) that government was completely unsuited to manage the lending of property. He acknowledged that

even were it possible to rectify the inequitable doings which have gone on during past thousands of years . . . the resulting state of things would be a less desirable one than the present . . . it suffices to remember the inferiority of public administration to private administration, to see that ownership by the state would work ill. Under the existing system of ownership, those who manage the land experience a direct connection between effort and benefit; while, were it under state ownership, those who managed it would experience no such direct connection. The vices of officialism would inevitably entail immense evils. (Spencer 1978, II, p. 460)

Coming back full square to his main political concern, by limiting state action Spencer was affirming the rights of individuals over their possessions. This was an obvious and necessary corollary of the law of equal freedom:

> When we assert the liberty of each bounded only by the like liberties of all, we assert that each is free to keep for himself all those gratifications and source of gratification which he procures without trespassing on the spheres of action of his neighbors. (Spencer 1978, II, p. 117)

The Limits of Corporate Capitalism

Some commentators have considered Herbert Spencer a foe of 'corporate capitalism,' by and large on the basis of an article he wrote on railways as corporations.[26] This judgement rests on the strong scepticism displayed by Spencer on features that may look distinctive of modern capitalism, particularly what has been called the 'separation of ownership and control.' Such an essay is of distinctive importance insofar as a railway company – because of his youthful work as a civil engineer – was unquestionably the only real world business Spencer knew intimately.

It needs to be clarified that, if the public company was the unchallenged protagonist of the history of capitalism in the twentieth century, joint-stock companies were a less defined object in Spencer's times. The financial markets were still too primitive to create the miracle behind modern capitalism: the fact that 'large companies control billions of dollars in resources raised from middle-class investors, whose contributions to insurance premium funds, and mutual funds pay for the stock that capitalizes' corporations all over the world, and primarily in the United States, the true homeland of the modern corporation (Macey 2009, p. 4).

To be sure, institutional devices to achieve risk sharing have long existed. Starting in medieval Italy and subsequently spreading to Europe, contract agreements were devised such as the *commenda* (an institute in which an investor, the *commendator*, advanced capital to a travelling associate, the *tractator*) and the *compagna*, which pooled together resources from different investors and was governed by a one-partner, one-vote system. By the sixteenth century, a corporation was already a legal person in English law, having certain rights, duties, and the power to perform legal actions.

Still, most of the advancements of the industrial revolution were undertaken by limited partnership. As noted by Ron Harris, by and large,

> the sole proprietorship, the family firm, and the closed partnership sufficed to meet the needs of the English economy. Only with the coming of the railway in the 1830s and 1840s did things change, and by then, the legal framework was responsive and the joint-stock corporation became readily available. (Harris 2000, p. 5)

It was precisely during the Victorian period that 'through a series of reforms to company law' it became 'much easier for large businesses to be incorporated as joint-stock companies with limited liability for their shareholders' (Casson and Godley 2010, p. 212).

One key feature of the modern corporation, limited liability, became more distinctive during the nineteenth century. Limited liability is considered an essential feature of corporations as it lowers transactions costs associated with issuing securities, therefore enabling better risk sharing and investment on a larger scale. As Easterbrook and Fishel put it,

> Limited liability does not eliminate ruin, and someone must bear losses when firms fail. [But] Limited liability is an arrangement under which the loss is swallowed rather than shifted. Each investor has a cap on the loss he will bear. (Easterbrook and Fishel 1991, p. 44)

The *Joint-Stock Company Act* of 1856 permitted companies to limit the liability of equity owners for the company's debts to be no greater than their initial investment (the Act excepted banking and insurance firms). Prior to 1856, limited liability could be obtained only by a special act of Parliament. The precedent that was followed was that of earlier chartered trading companies. These latter were seen with great suspicion by Adam Smith, who observed that

> the trade of a joint-stock company is always managed by a court of directors . . . The directors of such companies, however, being the managers rather of other people's money than of their own, it cannot well be expected, that they should watch over it with the same anxious vigilance with which the partners in a private copartnery frequently watch over their own. Like the stewards of a rich man, they are apt to consider attention to small matters as not for their master's honour, and very easily give themselves a dispensation from having it. Negligence and profusion, therefore, must always prevail, more or less, in the management of the affairs of such a company. It is upon this account that joint-stock companies for foreign trade have seldom been able to maintain the competition against private adventurers. They have, accordingly, very seldom succeeded without an exclusive privilege; and frequently have not succeeded with one. (Smith 1937, II, pp. 232–3)

Though acknowledging that 'some particular branches of commerce, which are carried on with barbarous and uncivilized nations, require extraordinary protection' (Smith 1937, II, p. 215), this denunciation of the unfair privileges granted to joint-stock companies being their only weapon to make profit is at the core of Smith's critique of mercantilism. Smith blamed them for 'playing the part of the sovereign at home by effectively capturing British state power and influencing trade to, and foreign policies about, America, Asia, and Africa' but also because they played 'the part of the sovereign in India' (Muthu 2008, p. 198). For Smith,

> The only trades which it seems possible for a joint-stock company to carry on successfully, without an exclusive privilege, are those, of which all the operations are capable of being reduced to what is called a routine, or to such a uniformity of method as admits of little or no variation. Of this kind is, first, the banking trade; secondly, the trade of insurance from fire, and from sea risk and capture in time of war; thirdly, the trade of making and maintaining a navigable cut or canal; and, fourthly, the similar trade of bringing water for the supply of a great city. (Smith 1937, II, p. 246)

Spencer discerned in the railway companies of his time much of what Smith saw in the international trade companies of his. The trade monopoly of the East India Company came to an end in 1813 for India and in 1833 for China, but Spencer saw a resurgence of mercantilism in the new transport industry. The latter was certainly instrumental for wealth creation to an unprecedented extent: until the advent of the railways, no one had travelled faster than a horse can gallop. By 1830 trains were thundering up and down England at the previously unimaginable speed of 60 mph. Few technological advancements ever modified commerce – and life at large – in such a rapid and unexpected way.

Railways were central in the regulatory history of the nineteenth century, being subject to regulatory acts in 1839 and 1844 and later being given limited liability in 1855. Railways and canals, as well as infrastructures generally speaking, were capital intensive and were therefore businesses that, in the need for capital, were well suited for incorporation and the attraction of a wide number of shareholders. Not surprisingly, 'provincial stock exchanges started to develop only in the 1830s and 1840s with the advance of the railway' (Harris 2000, p. 127).

The development of a railway company was by and large a *political effort*:

> Between 1830 and 1860 the promotion of a railway was usually undertaken by a small group of local citizens, anxious to connect their town to a local port or industrial city . . . They would organize a public meeting, chaired by a local dignitary, at which a motion supporting the railway scheme would be proposed . . . [then] a provisional committee would be formed with a mandate to secure an act of Parliament, until which time the committee would act as a 'shadow' board of directors. (Casson and Godley 2010, p. 233)

Spencer was thus particularly concerned – not unlike Adam Smith – with two different problems. One was the excessive proximity between these entrepreneurial organizations and the world of politics. The other was what he regarded as the respect for the original contracts binding the shareholders (i.e. he was preoccupied with excessive discretionary powers on the part of administrators and managers).

On the fist point, Spencer was concerned with 'increasing community between railway boards and the House of Commons' (Spencer 1854, pp. 74–5). Spencer cannot be but suspicious in front of a 'great change in the attitude of the Legislature towards railways,' from 'the extreme of determined rejection or dilatory acquiescence, to the opposite extreme of unlimited concession.'

On the second, in a nutshell, Spencer saw the possibility of exerting control on the part of shareholders as largely illusory, board elections being ineffective. He thought that the 'belief in the identity of directorial and proprietary interests, is the fatal error commonly made by shareholders' (Spencer 1854, p. 84).

He recommended that the contracts underpinning a railway should be more narrowly interpreted and more vigorously enforced as to compel shareholders to honor the specific purpose of incorporation.

Assuming that the contracts are themselves equitable, there is no rational system of ethics which warrants the alteration or dissolving of them, save by the consent of all concerned. If then it be shown, as we think it has been shown, that the contract tacitly entered into by railway shareholders with each other, has definite limits, it is the function of the Government to enforce, and not to abolish, those limits. (Spencer 1854, p. 96)

Railway companies represented a distinctive form of 'separation of ownership and control.' As Channon writes:

The men who were eventually responsible for designing the structures and procedures were not businessmen but salaried employees, managers in other words, who had little or no financial interest in the railway companies they served and who were not imbued with the values of 'personal' capitalism. (Channon 1999, p. 70)

For Spencer, the problem was 'the misinterpretation of the proprietary contract.' He maintained that managers and administrators often shifted from the original focus of the incorporation (this being less 'making railways' than 'making a particular railway'). Boards of directors and corporate managers engaged in ancillary businesses to the building of *a particular railway*, either in conscious mismanagement efforts or as political bargaining. Shareholders were impotent, being distant from management, dispersed in the country, and often naively unaware of the management's decisions. He feared the bureaucratization of joint-stock companies, where 'the plans of a board of directors are usually authorized with little or no discussion' (Spencer 1891, p. 24). He saw 'directorial power' as constantly risking to degenerate into 'oligarchy' and then into 'autocracy' (Spencer 1902, p. 244), with the result of making shareholders' property rights more and more vacuous.

Spencer saw this excessive empowerment of the administrators as the result of practices (including the vote by proxy) that resulted from the application of democratic rules to the polity of shareholders. He opposed the application of 'the doctrine of the will of the greater number' to companies, believing that proprietors could not be coerced by the will of fellow shareholders if that will contradicted the purposes on which they decided to unite and join in a contract.

Some commentators have argued that these passages in Spencer's writings suggest that – like other champions of free enterprise including Adam Smith – he displayed a level of distrust towards businesses and businessmen.[27]

But one key point in Spencer's reasoning suggests that he vehemently opposed the ideology that was constructed to support these efforts – a political formula that, strengthened by the development of Keynesianism in the twentieth century, actually survives to our day: the ideology of public works.

For Spencer, the ultimate test of the efficiency of any enterprise was the return on capital for investors. He persistently refused to accept the notion that building infrastructures should need subsidies, because the general good was to be estimated using a different measure than profits for shareholders. He reacted to the idea that 'undertakings which have been disastrous to shareholders' could be 'advantageous to the public,' assuming on the contrary that 'the interests of shareholders and the public are in end identical' (Spencer 1854, p. 103).

He felt outraged that a

large proportion of railway capital which does not pay the current rate of interest, is capital ill laid out . . . however true it may be that the sum invested in unprofitable lines will go on increasing in productiveness; yet, if more wisely invested, it would similarly have gone on increasing in productiveness, perhaps even at a greater rate, this vast loss must be regarded as a permanent and not as a temporary one . . . Money which, if used for a certain end, gives a smaller return than it would give if otherwise used, is used disadvantageously, not only to its possessors, but to the community. (Spencer 1854, pp. 102–3)

To be clear, 'this notion that railway enterprise will not go on with due activity without artificial incentives – that bills for local extensions "rather need encouragement", as the Committee says, is nothing but a remnant of protectionism' (Spencer 1854, p. 103).

It seems hard to legitimate the inference that Spencer would have opposed modern public companies on the basis of his view of the British nineteenth-century railway system. It is true that it is often maintained that, from the sixteenth century on, 'by granting the series of incorporations, the government implicitly assumed an active role within the marketplace, but in so doing set in place the legal structures necessary to promote the efficiency of the evolving corporate forms' (Gillman and Eade 1995, p. 28).

Still, the view that the roots of the modern corporation lie in state privilege is not unchallenged. Ekelund and Tollison have persuasively argued that 'careful scrutiny of pre-nineteenth-century business history demonstrates that the modern corporation developed and spread due to its superior economic efficiency as an organizational form, in spite of, not because of, governmental interference in the free market' (Ekelund and Tollison 1997, p. 209).

For our purposes, we should admit that Spencer's views on corporate governance were far from being inconsistent with his economic philosophy. It has to be stressed that for Spencer the principle of the 'law of conduct and consequence' was central. His preference for market arrangements was also motivated by the belief that markets were better in properly rewarding desert. This was at the base of his concerns for joint-stock companies: he did not want people to be undeservedly rewarded. But it was also at the root of his opinions about central banking and the world of finance. Vera Smith found Spencer's article on 'State tamperings with money and banks' (1858) among the very few significant contributions to the banking debate in England in the 1850s (Smith 1990, p. 82). In that essay, Spencer advanced the argument that 'the balance of a mixed currency of voluntary origin is, under all circumstances, self-adjusting,' stressing that in matters of banking 'all which the State has to do in the matter is to discharge its ordinary office – to administer justice.' If bankruptcy laws were to be properly enforced, the state should otherwise abstain from legislative meddling in this area, because 'the State can, and sometimes does, produce commercial disasters. As we shall also show, it can, and sometimes does, exacerbate the commercial disasters otherwise produced. But while it can create and can make worse, it cannot prevent' (Spencer 1858, p. 334).

The 'law of conduct and consequence' was a good policeman of social and economic life: Spencer was worried that improper interventions may just erode its effectiveness.

Divine Parliaments

The general attitude towards economic policy, and therefore the legitimacy of *laissez-faire* in the eyes of the public, changed decisively during Spencer's lifetime.

In the world of ideas, the belief in non-interventionism among the business class and leading economists declined sharply. Likewise, cultural critics (from Carlyle to novelists such as Dickens, Trollope and Thackeray) looked at industrial society with an increasing sense of foreboding, when they did not despise it altogether.

In the world of politics, starting from the establishment of universal male suffrage with the two Reform Acts of 1867 and 1884, the old 'social block' favouring free trade and non-intervention was little by little eaten away, and the political class came to support increasingly interventionist policies, apparently to the benefit of the newly enfranchised classes.

Herbert Spencer, the enthusiastic prophet of social evolution, was then confronted with the inconvenient truth that the world of social affairs was moving in a very different direction from the one he forecasted and in favour of which he preached. How did this affect his thinking and his views?

It would be a mistake to assume that Spencer thought of evolution as an inexorable process that followed an unswerving course. Spencer referred often to the importance of rhythm in evolution, in particular of the 'rhythm of motion': movement in one direction (i.e. in the direction of liberty and industrialism) could be balanced by counter-movement in the other. As he wrote in his *Autobiography*,

> On recognizing the universality of rhythm, it becomes clear that it was absurd to suppose that the great relaxation of restraints – political, social, commercial – which culminated in free trade would continue. A re-imposition of restraints, if not of the same kind, then of other kinds, was inevitable; and it is now manifest that whereas during a long period there had been an advance from involuntary cooperation in social affairs to voluntary cooperation [or, to use Sir Henry Maine's language, from status to contract], there has commenced a reversal of the process. (Spencer 1904, II, p. 369)

In the last phase of his life, Spencer came to the conclusion that

> It was absurd to suppose that the great relaxation of restraints – political, social, commercial – which culminated in free-trade, would continue. A re-imposition of restraints, if not of the same kind, then of other kinds, was inevitable; and it is now manifest that whereas during a long period there had been an advance from involuntary cooperation in social affairs to voluntary cooperation . . . there has now commenced a reversal of the process. (Spencer 1904, II, p. 369)

It has often been maintained that Spencer 'mutated' into a conservative guarantor of the status quo. This view is rooted in the fact he modified his views on the land question (as we have seen), on women rights, on democracy, and in the fact he eliminated the

chapter entitled 'The Right to Ignore the State' in the later ver-
sions of *Social Statics* (1868).

David Wiltshire remarked that '*Social Statics* (1851) contained
a triumphant and exhaustive affirmation of individual rights,
inalienable and inviolable. '*Justice*' (1891) largely repudiated
them . . . Spencer, the radical iconoclast of 1851, had become
the establishment philosopher of 1891, beloved of the Liberty
and Property Defence League' (Wiltshire 1978, pp. 161–2).
However, as Wiltshire himself noted, 'Spencer was consistent in
his dedication to individualism' (Wiltshire 1978, p. 271).

Did he really come to be a sort of 'establishment philosopher'?
For one thing, if Spencer was more famous in 1891 than in 1851,
he was hardly more attuned with the *Zeitgeist*. Spencer's aversion
to collectivism became more ardent with the passing of the years,
but then the menace of collectivism seemed to be more and
more real. If we consider political ideas and the political arena
to be somehow linked (as they obviously are), the British Liberal
Party was clearly more on Spencer's side in the 1850s than in the
1880s. Spencer didn't grow conservative: he grew *reactionary* –
that is, he strongly reacted against the betrayal of the political
ideas of his youth.

The question of whether and in what sense Spencer
changed his mind from his youth to later years will be with his
scholars for a long time. In a way, for an author whose intellectual production spans more than half a century, he showed
remarkable consistency. His preference for the free society,
market competition and individual liberty was unshaken for
all his life.

Spencer addressed the subject in the preface to the 1868
American edition of *Social Statics*, by honestly explaining that

during the fourteen years since the original publication of the
work, the general theory which it enunciates has undergone,
in his mind, [Spencer was referring to himself in third per-
son] considerable further development and some accompany-
ing modifications. So that, although he adheres to the leading

principles set forth in the following pages, he is not prepared
to abide by all the detailed applications of them. (Spencer
1868, p. vii)

When, in a letter, Spencer announced to Youmans the fact he
felt the need to add 'a brief prefatory' to the reprint of *Social
Statics*, he made clear likewise that he may have 'modified opinions on some points' but not 'receded from any of its [*Social
Statics*'s] main principles' (Duncan 1908, I, pp. 145–6). Spencer
further clarified that

no essential changes of the views set forth in Social Statics
proved needful; but there came to be recognized a deeper
origin for its fundamental principles. The assertion of the liberty of each limited only by the like liberties of all, was shown
to imply the doctrine that each ought to receive the benefits
and bear the evils entailed by his actions . . . this ultimate principle of social conduct was affiliated upon the general process
of organic evolution. (Spencer 1899, p. 364)

Perhaps, as he wrote in his *Autobiography*, looking back at his
1850s writings, 'my confidence in the rationality of mankind was
much greater than it is now' (Spencer 1904, II, p. 50).

It is true that, in the words of Ellen Frankel Paul, Herbert
Spencer was 'the philosopher who mourned the death of the
"Old Liberalism" more acutely than any of his contemporaries'
(Paul 1980, p. 66). But he did so because he saw better than
others how the political ideals of his youth were at stake – in the
wake of the emergence of mass politics.

Spencer never abandoned the law of equal freedom as the
cornerstone of his beliefs: 'the liberty which a citizen enjoys is to
be measured, not by the nature of the governmental machine
he lives under . . . but by the relative paucity of the restraints it
imposes on him' (Spencer 1981, p. 79). But he saw that these
restraints were actually to grow, and not be reduced, with the
enlargement of the franchise.[28]

His reaction was chiefly directed against the second Gladstone government (that he credited with substantially growing the sphere of public powers) and against those intellectuals who favoured, from an ostensibly liberal stance, such a course. This turned the Liberals into 'the new Tories.' If historically the liberals aim to diminish 'compulsory cooperation throughout social life' and increase 'voluntary cooperation' to diminish governmental authority and increase 'the area in which each citizen may act unchecked,' now the 'new' Liberals acted in the opposite direction (Spencer 1981, p. 10).

The new Liberals, Spencer charged, forgot the animating core of their beliefs – that is, individual freedom as opposed to state coercion – and rather than seeking to enable the public good by indirect, market means, and by relaxing restraints on individual enterprise, they began to search for easy fixes, for direct, governmental means to advance the social good. A curious phenomenon occurred, then: for precisely when social evils decreased, the denunciation of these same evils increased, and the public began demanding the therapeutic intervention of the state. Each piece of meddlesome legislation served as precedent, increasing the momentum for further regulation, and Spencer became increasingly pessimistic, convinced that Britain was ineluctably slipping into a new age of feudalistic militarism. Then came the 'new Tories,' preaching a 'benevolent' enlargement of compulsory cooperation, to the expense of voluntary cooperation,[29] for 'as fast as the régime of contract is discarded, the régime of status is of necessity adopted. As fast as voluntary cooperation is abandoned, compulsory cooperation must be substituted' (Spencer 1981, p. 14). The same view that came to predominate in earlier stages of evolution, when it was used to strengthen the power of the kings, was now paradoxically to become the cement of democratic theory.

This implied a change in the *political methods* of Liberals too. As it was summarized by Albert J. Nock (1870–1945), a crucial difference was that 'the early Liberal proceeded towards the realization of his aims by the method of repeal. He was not for making new laws, but for repealing old ones' (Nock 1981, p. xxv).

This change of method was a change in substance. From the standpoint of the law of equal freedom, it is clearly different to take active part in politics with the aim of restricting the sphere of action of the state and to do the same with the goal of enlarging the scope of state's action. Such a change in method, Spencer noted, was largely due to the triumph of the democratic procedure.[30] This happened in two ways: the broadened franchise changed the constituency of the government, leading to the emergence of new political demands. But also, a larger franchise gave symbolically a sort of a blank cheque to political power.

Even in his youth Spencer embraced a qualified theory of democracy. 'His early politics reflected the nuances of the defence of civil liberty, not that of consent-based democracy' (Francis 2007, p. 272). His acceptance of democracy was subordinated to the acceptance of what he called 'the right to ignore the state' (i.e. voluntary citizenship):

> Government being simply an agent employed in common by a number of individuals to secure to them certain advantages, the very nature of the connection implies that it is for each to say whether he will employ such an agent or not. (Spencer 1995, p. 185)

In *Social Statics*, to be 'the only one admissible' a purely democratic government needed two conditions: citizenship should be voluntary and 'it shall confer equal privileges' (Spencer 1995, p. 195), including voting rights.

For one thing, majority rule was already a 'political superstition' for the young Spencer (Spencer 1995, p. 188). In his system, 'the enactment of public arrangements by vote . . . implies that the desires of some cannot be satisfied without sacrificing the desires of others . . . implies that in the pursuit of their happiness the majority inflict a certain amount of unhappiness on the minority' (Spencer 1995, p. 189).

As we have seen, for the young Spencer who authored *The Proper Sphere of Government*, equal shares in the administration of government were acceptable and indeed rightful, insofar as government was properly limited. He rejected the paternalistic arguments against democracy (the people will be too ignorant to take meaningful political decisions) precisely because he assumed that in a democratic state the scope of collective choice would be strictly limited. Paucity of state actions did support democracy, in his view: the state being concerned with the fundamental issue of the administration of justice, voting one way or another cannot have the effect of bringing the government to act against the law of equal freedom, restraining the freedom of action, or seizing the property of some to the benefit of others.

In later years, Spencer actually blamed himself for not having understood ahead of the time that extending the franchise 'would result in replacing the old class legislation by a new class legislation' (Spencer 1904, II, p. 366). The extension of the franchise, by dissociating 'the giving of votes from the bearing of burdens,' was to be followed inevitably by a 'still more rapid growth of socialistic legislation' (Spencer 1904, II, p. 56).

The idea that 'Government should step in whenever anything is not going right' (Spencer 1981, p. 46) was gaining momentum. Spencer saw this growth of government intervention as disastrous in many ways. For one thing, behind this new wave of regulation was the view that the 'regulative policy' of society could be superseded: the 'law of conduct and consequence' could be amended by legislative fiat, an artificial order could be substituted for the natural one. But from another point of view, 'every extension of regulative policy involves an addition to the regulative agents' (Spencer 1981, p. 47). The growth of 'officialism,' in Spencer's words, necessarily means what now we may call the bureaucratization of society.

The extension of democracy played an important role in this process. The popular masses that were entering the political scene were educated with 'extensive reading of publications which foster pleasant illusions' and therefore were brought to 'nurture sanguine anticipations of benefits to be obtained by social reorganization,' with the result that 'whoever seeks their votes must at least refrain from exposing their mistaken beliefs' (Spencer 1981, p. 51).[31]

The masses were thus deluded that increased state actions could be only beneficial, but, wrote Spencer, anticipating Milton Friedman's (1902–2006) warning that there is no such thing as a free lunch, 'what looks like a gratis benefit is not a gratis benefit' (Spencer 1981, p. 37). Entitlements awarded via government redistributions needed to be financed by taxation, which was in turn to have an impact on the working poor. The arguments, some forty years later, were exactly the same used in *The Proper Sphere of Government* against the Poor Law.

But Spencer's reflections on the symbolic dimension of politics were even more illuminating. He understood that the 'great political superstition of the past was the divine right of kings. The great superstition of the present is the divine right of parliaments' (Spencer 1981, p. 123). The divine right of parliaments means 'the divine right of majorities. The fundamental assumption made by legislators and people alike, is that a majority has powers which have no bounds' (Spencer 1981, p. 129). In one thing, Spencer never changed his mind: he could sense the tension (later thematized by Elie Halevy) between the tendency, in utilitarian thought, to identify the general interest with 'the providential intervention of a legislator' and the understanding of the free economy as spontaneously harmonizing individual interests.[32] This fundamental compromise was at the root of the new Liberals' treason: utilitarian thinkers found themselves so fond of legislation, they came to ultimately hold the view that a democratic assembly should have unrestricted power over its subjects.

To be sure, Spencer was not the first liberal to be sceptical of the universal franchise. John Stuart Mill had great concerns about the effect of representative democracy on human freedom. Alexis de Tocqueville (1805–59) feared likewise the cultural by-products of democracy. Authors as different as Benjamin Constant and Antonio Rosmini (1797–1855) expressed their preference for a qualified franchise. Wilhelm von Humboldt (1767–1835), whose *The Limits of State's Action* inspired Mill's *On Liberty*, noted that the legitimacy of political institutions is based upon

> the necessity of securing the consent of every individual. But this very necessity renders the decision by a majority of voices impossible; and yet no other could be thought in the case of a state which extended its activity to include the positive welfare of the citizen. Nothing would be left to the unconsenting but to withdraw from the community in order to escape its jurisdiction, and prevent the further application of a majority suffrage to their individual case. (Humboldt 1993, p. 36)

Still, Spencer was one of the few who understood the symbolic dimension of democratic rule. He saw that if 'the rule of everybody' became a political superstition, it could open the door to unprecedented state powers. He feared the idea that political decisions could be considered 'sacred' just because the *locus* of political decision was changing from the court to a democratic assembly. He rightly forecasted the future of classical liberalism: 'the function of Liberalism in the past was that of putting a limit to the powers of kings. The function of true Liberalism in the future will be that of putting a limit to the powers of Parliaments' (Spencer 1981, p. 166).

Herbert Spencer, Our Contemporary

Bruno Leoni remarked that Spencer anticipated 'very often in the smallest detail' (Leoni 2008, p. 105) twentieth-century criticisms of socialism.

This statement is to be considered particularly in the light of Spencer's criticism of democracy as conducive to greater and greater social intervention (as we saw above), but also on a number of other issues that actually bring Spencer closer to some of the unquestioned masters of classical liberalism in the twentieth century – among others, F. A. Hayek.

Spencer can be credited with a deep understanding of the two phenomena whose unprecedented growth characterized the twentieth century: taxation and legislation. In this realm, the quintessential feature of Spencer's way of looking at the world is his *realism*. A thorough critic of 'political superstitions,' including majority rule, Spencer never imagined decisions of the political class could be 'neutral.' He clearly understood that taxation and regulation entail winners and losers, the first being typically interest groups limited in size, the other being the vast majority of citizens.

His very evolutionary theory, which produced the two types society – military and industrial – somehow embodied a global view of society that differentiated between those individuals who, being in government, had coercive powers at hand, and those who, instead, lived on their ability to satisfy each other's needs in contractual agreements. This fundamental distinction somehow encompasses modes of cooperation and juridical arrangements between society's members (contract and status), but also classes of human beings.

This is apparent in the 'Tale of the Slave' that Robert Nozick (1938–2002) used in his *Anarchy, State, and Utopia* (Nozick 1974, pp. 291–2) to explain taxation. It is worth quoting this passage at length. In *Man Versus the State*, Spencer proclaimed that 'all socialism involves slavery' and explained:

What is essential to the idea of a slave? We primarily think of him as one who is owned by another. To be more than nominal, however, the ownership must be shown by control of the slave's actions – a control which is habitually for the benefit of the controller. That which fundamentally distinguishes the slave is that he labours under coercion to satisfy another's desires. The relation admits of sundry gradations. Remembering that originally the slave is a prisoner whose life is at the mercy of his captor, it suffices here to note that there is a harsh form of slavery in which, treated as an animal, he has to expend his entire effort for his owner's advantage. Under a system less harsh, though occupied chiefly in working for his owner, he is allowed a short time in which to work for himself, and some ground on which to grow extra food. A further amelioration gives him power to sell the produce of his plot and keep the proceeds. Then we come to the still more moderated form which commonly arises where, having been a free man working on his own land, conquest turns him into what we distinguish as a serf; and he has to give to his owner each year a fixed amount of labour or produce, or both: retaining the rest himself. Finally, in some cases, as in Russia before serfdom was abolished, he is allowed to leave his owner's estate and work or trade for himself elsewhere, under the condition that he shall pay an annual sum. What is it which, in these cases, leads us to qualify our conception of the slavery as more or less severe? Evidently the greater or smaller extent to which effort is compulsorily expended for the benefit of another instead of for self-benefit. If all the slave's labour is for his owner the slavery is heavy, and if but little it is light. Take now a further step. Suppose an owner dies, and his estate with its slaves comes into the hands of trustees; or suppose the estate and everything on it to be bought by a company; is the condition of the slave any the better if the amount of his compulsory labour remains the same? Suppose that for a company we substitute the community; does it make any difference to the slave if the time he has to work for others is as great, and the time left for himself is as small, as before? The essential question is – How much is he compelled to labour for other benefit than his own, and how much can he labour for his own benefit? The degree of his slavery varies according to the ratio between that which he is forced to yield up and that which he is allowed to retain; and it matters not whether his master is a single person or a society. If, without option, he has to labour for the society, and receives from the general stock such portion as the society awards him, he becomes a slave to the society. Socialistic arrangements necessitate an enslavement of this kind; and towards such an enslavement many recent measures, and still more the measures advocated, are carrying us. Let us observe, first, their proximate effects, and then their ultimate effects. (Spencer 1981, pp. 55–7)

Nozick turned this into a story, describing ten steps from slavery to a situation in which 'the master allows all of his 10,000 slaves, except you, to vote, and the joint decision is made by all of them.' Nozick effectively explained taxation as a form of slavery by using an example grabbed from Spencer. Both understood taxation as intrinsically coercive: 'takings' from single individuals that could not simply be understood as fees paid for the provision of a public good, or as a 'club membership' in society.

Likewise, one of Spencer's most famous articles is titled after one of the great evils of contemporary statism: overlegislation. For Robert Nisbet, 'Overlegislation' was the single article to read to acquire 'an accurate and full appreciation of Spencer's liberalism' (Nisbet 1980, p. 231). This article is 'at once a powerful affirmation of individual freedom as the only freedom worth considering and a demonstration of the intrinsic incapacity of the political state to deal effectively or justly with any social or moral problem.' Spencer's dissection of administration, Nisbet noted, was 'merciless but, by any rational standard, including that of Max Weber, perceptive and fair' (Nisbet 1980, p. 232).

The article is imbued with what we may call 'political realism,' which is apparent in Spencer's assessment of the working of a government bureaucracy: though Spencer does not develop a refined vision of the system of incentives underpinning the conduct of bureaucrats, he simply considers politicians, regulators and bureaucrats to be as self-interested as any other human beings:

All the actions going on in society come under the generalization: human efforts ministering to human desire. Whether the ministration be effected through a process of buying and selling, or whether in any other way, matters not so far as the general law of it is concerned. (Spencer 1853, p. 314)

Identical men inhabit the public and the private world, but they face different incentives. What makes bureaucracy 'slow,' 'stupid' and 'extravagant' is the fact it operates in a condition of monopoly. The system of 'officialism' (as he calls the bureaucracy and by doing so, highlights its formalistic nature) is composed of public agencies that 'are subject to no such influence as that which obliges private enterprise to be economical. Traders and mercantile bodies succeed by serving society cheaply. Such of them as cannot do this are continually supplanted by those who can.'

A private firm is forced towards efficiency by *competition*: in a free market, only the fittest survive and prosper, but this is not the case in a system in which adaptiveness, thrift and intelligence are not properly rewarded.

> Under the natural course of things each citizen tends towards his fittest function. Those who are competent to the kind of work they undertake, succeed, and, in the average of cases, are advanced in proportion to their efficiency; while the incompetent, society soon finds out, ceases to employ, forces to try something easier, and eventually turns to use. But it is quite otherwise in State-organizations. (Spencer 1853, p. 287)

The lack of the 'antiseptic' of free competition is the cause of the 'invariable corruption' of bureaucracies.

Why is the state bound to inefficiency? Spencer finds the answer in the selection mechanism in the public world, so different from the sharp rule of meritocracy employed in private business. In bureaucratic bodies, 'as every one knows . . . birth, age, backstairs intrigue, and sycophancy, determine the selections rather than merit' (Spencer 1853, p. 287).

Wherever there is government there is villainy. It is the inevitable result of destroying the direct connection between the profit obtained and the work performed. No incompetent person hopes, by offering a *douceur* in *The Times*, to get a permanent place in a mercantile office. But where, as under government, there is no employers' self-interest to forbid; where the appointment is made by someone on whom the inefficient entails no loss; there a *douceur* is operative . . . In State organizations . . . corruption is unavoidable. (Spencer 1853, p. 292)

The 'law of conduct and consequence' is suspended in the public realm, so to say, and the obvious result of this denial of freedom and responsibility, is the rule of privilege.

Quite realistically, Spencer understood this to be a typical phenomenon of social aggregates. Later on, by forecasting the impending 'tyranny of the bureaucracies' (Spencer 1981, p. 23), he thought it was worth generalizing the fact that 'regulative structure always tends to increase in power' (Spencer 1981, p. 24). Spencer saw this trend as truly pervasive: emerging in governments, in joint-stock companies (as we saw), and even in trade unions. Without attaining the precise formulation of Michels's 'iron law of oligarchy,' but still a few years ahead, Spencer observed that

already, in the general organization of Trade Unions so recently formed, there are complaints of 'wire-pullers' and 'bosses' and 'permanent officials.' If, then, this supremacy of the regulators is seen in bodies of quite modern origin, formed of men who have . . . unhindered powers of asserting their independence, what will the supremacy of the regulators become in long-established bodies, in bodies which have grow vast and highly organized, and in bodies which, instead of controlling only a small part of the unit's life, control the whole of his life? (Spencer 1891, p. 25)

This statement should not be read as an indictment of
Spencer's broader account of evolution moving to industrialism
and spontaneous cooperation from militancy. He regarded 'the
present social state' as 'transitional,' and he did not renounce his
evolutionary views. He considered statism 'a constitution inherited from primitive men' (Spencer 1891, p. 31), and thought
that men should adapt to the true conditions of industrialism.

Actually, Spencer's understanding of bureaucracies as inherently inefficient is based on his parallel appreciation of market
mechanisms as *spontaneous orders*. 'Overlegislation' is a powerful
and beautifully written essay; the style seems more that of
the vibrant polemicist than one of the thoughtful writer: the
entire argument there is played on the opposition between
non-spontaneous and spontaneous entities, with the latter being
the benchmark against which the former are evaluated. In the
tour de force[33] of his arguments, Spencer explains how one of
the true vices of officialism is its 'unadaptiveness.'

> Unlike private enterprise which quickly modifies its actions to
> meet emergencies; unlike the shopkeeper who promptly finds
> the wherewith to satisfy a sudden demand; unlike the railway
> company which doubles its trains to carry a special influx of
> passengers; the law-made instrumentality lumbers on under
> all varieties of circumstances through its ordained routine at
> its habitual rate. By its very nature it is fitted only for average
> requirements, and inevitably fails under unusual requirements.
> (Spencer 1853, p. 289)

Here Spencer becomes a true contemporary of ours: because
his most poignant argument against over-regulation rests basically on the nature of *complexity*. As consistent with Spencer's
theory, any change in the world demands rapid adaptation.
Rapid adaptation implies not only quick decision-making procedures, but requires a grasping of the social conditions in which
somebody intervenes. Alas, our cognitive possibilities are limited and powerless in front of the complexities of social matters.

It is because 'I am struck with the incompetence of my intellect to prescribe for society' (Spencer 1853, p. 267) that Spencer thought it necessary 'to question the propriety of meddling' with the spontaneous course of social and economic affairs.

For this very reason, Spencer was deeply sceptical of the very logic still underpinning many justifications for state actions; for example, in limiting the impact of externalities, or providing public goods that supposedly cannot be provided by private companies acting in a free market. Shortcomings on the part of the free market as far as concerns providing 'pure air, more knowledge, good water' are assumed to be permanent, but some men, per se as fallible as private citizens, are considered apt to solve these problems, by the virtue of constructing 'agencies of this same defective humanity that acts so ill' (Spencer 1853, p. 274).

'In their efforts to cure specific evils, legislators have continually caused collateral evils they never looked for' (Spencer 1853, p. 282); unintended consequences played a vital role in Spencer's view. Legislators, being limited, cannot wrestle with the fact that 'each phenomenon is a link in an infinite series, is the result of a myriad of preceding phenomena, and will have a share in producing myriads of succeeding ones.' In 'disturbing any natural chain of sequences, they are not only modifying the result next in succession, but all the future results into which this will enter as a part-cause' (Spencer 1853, p. 280). 'The social organism cannot be dealt with in any one part without all other parts being influenced in ways which cannot be foreseen' (ibidem).

In the *Study of Sociology* (Spencer 1873, p. 270) Spencer asked, 'is humanity more readily straightened than an iron plate?' He condemned social engineering on the grounds that any introduction of a new piece of legislation had unintended consequences: 'in proportion as an aggregate is complex, the effects wrought by an incident force become more multitudinous, confused and incalculable.' A society is 'of all kinds of aggregates the kind most difficult to affect in intended and not in unintended ways.'

Of course, social engineers typically assumed that 'functionaries are trustworthy' as their first postulate, but then 'doubtless could good officers be ensured, much might be said for officialism; just as despotism would have its advantages, could we ensure a good despot' (Spencer 1853, p. 295).

No matter how refined their arguments could seem, for Spencer all faith in governmental fiat as resolutive of social problems rested on an atavism: its roots could be traced back to the time when 'rulers were thought demi-gods' (Spencer 1853, p. 329). 'All superstitions die hard; and we fear that this belief in government omnipotence will form no exception.' He might have been forgotten and even despised, but Herbert Spencer was certainly right on this point.

Notes

[1] Miall was a major political figure too: in 1844, he was one of the founders of the British Anti-State-Church Association, that was renamed in 1853 the Society for the Liberation of Religion from State Patronage and Control, known for short as the Liberation Society. A Parliamentary member for the Liberal Party for Rochdale (1852–7) and Bradford (1860–74), he led the long fight for the abolition of compulsory churchrates that was finally successful in 1868.

[2] It should be noted that Conway uses a formula that can be traced back to what Herbert Spencer, in *Social Statics*, called 'the law of equal liberty.'

[3] As Albert V. Dicey wrote,

> The theory of free trade won by degrees the approval of statesmen of special insight, and adherents to the new economic religion were one by one gained among persons of intelligence. Cobden and Bright finally become potent advocates of truths of which they were in no sense the discoverers. This assertion in no way detracts from the credit due to these eminent men. They performed to admiration the proper function of popular leaders; by prodigies of energy, and by seizing a favourable opportunity, of which they made the very most use that was possible, they gained the acceptance by the English people of truths which have rarely, in any country but England, acquired popularity (Dicey 1905, p. 24).

[4] The role played by ideas and education in the abolition of the Corn Laws can hardly be underestimated, but those of a more materialistic persuasion may still take a sceptical view. See, for example, George Stigler (1911–91) who ridiculed the idea that the abolition of the Corn Laws was brought by anything else than historical necessity:

> I believe that if Cobden had spoken only Yiddish, and with a stammer, and Peel had been a narrow, stupid man, England would have moved toward free trade in grain as its agricultural classes declined and its manufacturing and commercial classes grew. Perhaps a few years later, but not many. In 1846, the agricultural classes in England had fallen to about one-fourth of the labor force. Truly effective import prohibitions would have driven grain to intolerable price levels, and intolerable things are not tolerated. (Stigler 1975)

[5] Robert Nisbet has polemically – albeit graciously – noted that

> no one, not St. Augustine, not Joachim de Fiore, not any of the millenarians of the Puritan Revolution, had invoked the idea of necessity, of necessary movement toward a given goal, with greater, more dogmatic certainty than does the rationalist-secularist Spencer. (Nisbet 1980, p. 235)

[6] On the idea that evolution occurs by differentiation, Spencer himself acknowledges the influence of K. E. von Baer (1792–1876), a Baltic German naturalist who studied embryology and maintained that the embryo, in its development from a single cell to an animal, becomes increasingly complex thru differentiation. Baer believed that 'ontogeny recapitulates phylogeny,' that is, the development of an organism does somehow recapitulate early stages in the development of its species.

[7] For a far more nuanced view of the tensions between Spencer's individualism and organicism, see T. S. Gray (1996). For the opposite thesis, placing Spencer in the organicist camp, see Francis (2007).

[8] As is well known, Thomas Huxley accused Spencer of inconsistency between his evolutionary theory and his preference for small government because

> the higher the state of civilisation, the more completely do the actions of one member of the social body influence all the rest, and the less possible it is for any one man to do a wrong thing without interfering, more or less, with the freedom of all his fellow-citizens. So that, even upon the narrowest view of the functions of the State, it must be admitted to have wider powers. (Huxley 1891, p. 261)

Spencer replied with an essay on 'Specialized Administration' in which he carved in the evolutionary jargon the basic distinction between government and society, referring to his theme of militancy versus industrialism. Spencer distinguished between positively regulative functions and negatively regulative functions of government, the latter being strengthened insofar as social evolution took place (moving towards industrialism), the former belonging to previous states of development in which the state intruded, by and large, into people's lives. For an interesting reading of the context of the debate between Huxley and Spencer, see Elwick (2003).

[9] Ironically enough, those believing war to be a sort of 'hygiene of the world' would most likely be labelled 'social Darwinists' today, instead of anti-militarists such as Spencer and William Graham Sumner (1840–1910).

[10] Spencer was an adamant opponent of national education throughout his life. This was consistent with his pedagogic teachings, which emphasized the importance of free learning and play. But Spencer likewise thought that any governmental attempt to foster education was to result in a coercive harmonization of society. He always contested the government's 'right to impose its system of culture upon the citizen, may be moulded after its approved pattern' (Spencer 1902, p. 83).

[11] It has been noted that the idea that men need to adapt to the world, since the latter was designed to bring about human happiness, was taken by Spencer from phrenological naturalism – in particular, from George Combe (1788–1858). *The Constitution of Man* by Combe was a true nineteenth-century best-seller, of which thousands of copies were distributed.

[12] As Taylor notes, 'Mill had a point: while Spencer might regard pleasure as the ultimate good, he rejected most other aspects that were generally associated with utilitarian moral theory' (2007, p. 111).

[13] In his review in *The Economist*, Thomas Hodgskin appreciated and praised this refutation of the theory of expediency, finding Spencer's vehement rebuttal of Benthamism uplifting. He was himself convinced that 'positive law . . . is the negation of natural law and, in particular, of the right of property' (Halevy 1956, p. 163). The review was published in *The Economist* on 8 Feb 1851 (pp. 149–51).

[14] Curiously, Spencer himself found the book the best written of his, blaming a certain decline in the quality of his writing style to the fact from the mid-1850s on he relied on an amanuensis. He found dictating easy but believed it negatively affected his prose (see Spencer 1904, II, pp. 35–6).

[15] An investigation of Spencer's relationship with religion is beyond the scope of this work. For our purposes, it may suffice to say that, after *Social Statics*, Spencer's "breezy deism" mutated into "a simple agnosticism which was still, despite Spencer's continued opposition to the 'theological party,' deeply conciliatory towards religion" (Peel 1971, pp. 127–28).

Spencer came to consider that all dogmatic religious options are unacceptable but share a grain of truth: beyond the phenomena that we know, there is an Unknowable Power. Human reason, being limited, cannot dare to grasp the absolute: in a way, in Spencer the dismissal of religion is complemented by an attempt to allow for the survival of a "religious sense" of some sort.

This may help in explaining why Spencer's attempts to deal with the problems of religion became more and more 'sociological' with the passing of time. "(. . .) I have come more and more to look calmly on forms of religious belief to which I had, in earlier days, a pronounced aversion. Holding that they are in the main naturally adapted to their respective people and times, it now seems to me well that they should severally live and work as long as the conditions permit, and, further, that sudden changes of religious institutions (. . .) are certain to be followed by reactions" (1904, II, p. 468).

However, Spencer remained clear that "if it be asked why, thinking thus, I have persevered in getting forth views at variance with current creeds, my reply is (. . .): it is for each to utter that which he sincerely believes to be true and, adding his unit of influence to all other units, leave the results to work themselves out" (1904, II, p. 469).

[16] As Spencer himself noted, evolution was not a word he used yet, but he commented that 'acceptance of the developmental idea had been tacit only; but soon after the publication of *Social Statics* it was avowed' by the publishing of the 'Development Hypothesis' in 1853.

[17] The distinction between 'absolute' and 'relative' ethics could bear significant problems of interpretation, as already pointed out by Maitland (1911).

[18] A person 'cannot be coerced into political combination without a breach of the law of equal freedom; he can withdraw from it without committing any such breach, and he has the right to do so' (Spencer 1995, p. 185).

[19] In his *Autobiography* Spencer considers it 'the strangest and most indefensible' doctrine in *Social Statics*, (Spencer 1904, I, p. 362), basically because of the problem of free-riding: there is no way, Spencer maintained, to exit from a political community without keeping to

benefit from basic public goods (protection from foreign attacks, internal police) supplied from the government.

[20] Herbert Spencer was far from alone in recognizing that sophistication of the division of labour in society brought with itself the possibility of a wider differentiation among individuals. Far from sharing Spencer's ideological passions, another of the founding fathers of sociology, Emile Durkheim (1858–1917) recognized that 'the more primitive societies are, the more resemblances there are among the individuals who compose them' (Durkheim 1964, p. 133). Durkheim noted that

> solidarity which comes from likeness is at its maximum when the collective conscience completely envelops our whole conscience and coincides in all points with it. But, at that moment, our individuality is nil . . . It is quite otherwise with the solidarity which the division of labour produces. Whereas the previous type implies that individuals resemble each other, this type presumes their difference . . . the activity of each is as much more personal as it is more specialized. (Durkheim 1964, pp. 130–1)

[21] Was Spencer guilty of a 'historicist fallacy'? See the debate between Paul (1982) and Taylor (1989).

[22] More broadly, a

> truly anti-imperialist political philosophy emerges in the late eighteenth century among a broad array of thinkers from different intellectual and national contexts. For economic reasons of free trade, from principles of self-determination or cultural integrity, due to concerns about the effects of imperial politics upon domestic political institutions and practices, and sometimes driven by contempt over the ironic spectacle of ostensibly free nations engaging in despotism, corruption and lawlessness abroad, a significant group of European political thinkers rejected imperialism outright as unworkable, dangerous or immoral. (Muthu 1999, p. 4)

[23] For an introduction to themes of left-libertarianism, see, for example Otsuka (2003), as well as Vallentyne and Steiner (2000).

[24] George (1892) reacted against Spencer's volte-face, identifying him as an example of "intellectual prostitution" (George 1892, p.272).

[25] Spencer did not come to see, then, the problems that common land ownership could represent for the law of equal freedom. On the ground of the law of equal freedom, Paul has persuasively demonstrated that applying the law of equal freedom to the availability of land would result in a very unstable equilibrium (Paul 1982, p. 512). In Spencer's scheme, the use of land by a single individual would be

based on a lease, to which society in its complexity would have consented. But then, what about new inhabitants? Any single newborn would basically make the previous equilibrium in the distribution of land once more untenable, according to the law of equal freedom.

[26] The other article commonly referred to is Spencer (1859), in which he condemns excessive desire for wealth as 'the great inciter' of malpractices. He also highlights limited knowledge as the source of many mistakes committed by all-powerful boards of directors of joint-stock companies.

[27] In addition to his speech at Delmonico's against 'the gospel of work,' in *The Principles of Ethics* it is suggested that as a matter of self-restraint or negative benevolence 'anyone who, by command of great capital or superior business capacity, is enabled to beat others who carry on the same business, is enjoined by the principle of negative beneficence to restrain his business activities, when his own wants and those of his belongings have been abundantly fulfilled; and so others, occupied as he is, may fulfill their wants also, though in smaller measure' (Spencer 1978, II, p. 302). However, it needs to be stressed that Spencer wasn't asking for any regulatory constraint against predatory practices, or just 'tough business' (or the survival of fittest among enterprises), but was just proposing a principle of self-restraint.

[28] More controversial appears to be the issue of the rights of women, even though it is related to the issue of enfranchisement. In *Social Statics*, Spencer came to endorse an almost 'feminist' position; it was remarked that he

> has shown that the status of women and children improves in proportion to the decline of militarism and the advance of industrialism. The military spirit is encouraged in multifold ways by both church and state, and little children and women, in their pitiable ignorance, assist in weaving nets that shall trip their own unwary feet and those of other women and children that follow them. (Dixon Davidson 1892)

In *Social Statics*, Spencer proclaimed that

> the rights of women must stand or fall with those of men, derived as they are from the same authority . . . the law of equal freedom applies alike to both sexes . . . subordination of females to males has to be repudiated, because it implies the use of command and thereby reveals it descent from barbarism. (Spencer 1995, pp. 152–3)

In later years, Spencer came to believe that women were to be excluded from the franchise so long as there was 'partial militancy,' since they were exempt from military duties (Spencer 1978, II, p. 194). He also came to regard the difference between the sexes, because of what he considered female impulsiveness and female tendency to prefer 'generosity over justice' (because of their nature having been modelled over family duties) as a factor bringing women to favour excessive state interventions.

[29] A very unlikely companion of Spencer in bringing together Tourism and socialism, was G. B. Shaw who happened to write (and with approbation) that

> all socialists are Tories in that sense. The Tory is a man who believes that those who are qualified by nature and training for public work, and who are naturally a minority, have to govern the mass of the people. That is Tourism. That is also Bolshevism. (Shaw 1921, p. 15)

[30] In other circumstances, Spencer focused on the effects of increased aggressiveness in foreign policy, on the evolution of societies:

> If we contrast the period from 1815 to 1850 with the period from 1850 to the present time, we cannot fail to see that along with increased armaments, more frequent conflicts, and revived military sentiment, there has been a spread of compulsory regulations. While nominally extended by the giving of votes, the freedom of the individual has been in many ways actually diminished; both by restrictions which ever-multiplying officials are appointed to insist on, and by the forcible taking of money to secure for him, or others at his expense, benefits previously left to be secured by each for himself. (Spencer 1882, p. 587)

A fellow 'founding father of sociology,' Vilfredo Pareto (1848–1923) observed that the same phenomenon Spencer referred to here, manifested itself in the wake of the First World War (Pareto 1922, p. 1145). Pareto knew Spencer's writings very well and, though with age he became increasingly critical towards some of their aspects, he could certainly be enrolled among Spencer's admirers.

[31] Spencer thought that the survival of free institutions was due far more to 'character' (a peculiarly Victorian concept) than to 'education.' He thought that

> not lack of information, but lack of certain moral sentiment, is the root of the evil . . . free institutions can be properly worked only by men, each of whom is jealous of his own rights, and also sympa-

thetically jealous of the rights of others, who will neither himself aggress on his neighbours in small things nor tolerate aggression on them by others. (Spencer 1883, pp. 476, 477)

[32] For a brilliant treatment of this issue, see Halevy (1966, pp. 487–91).

[33] Spencer comes to write that those who advocate greater and greater state involvement in societal affairs are blind to empirical evidence. They perhaps

> read backwards the parable of the talents. Not to the agent of proved efficiency do they consign further duties, but to the negligent and blundering agent. Private enterprise has done much, and done it well. Private enterprise has cleared, drained, and fertilized the country, and built the towns; has excavated mines, laid out roads, dug canals, and embanked railways; has invented, and brought to perfection ploughs, looms, steam engines, printing presses, and machines innumerable; has built our ships, our vast manufactories, our docks; has established banks, insurance societies, and the newspaper press; has covered the sea with lines of steam-vessels, and the land with electric telegraphs . . . On the other hand, the state so fulfils its judicial function as to ruin many, delude others, and frighten away those who most need succour; its national defences are so extravagantly and yet inefficiently administered as to call forth almost daily complaint, expostulation, or ridicule; and as the nation's steward, it obtains from some of our vast public estates a minus revenue. Therefore, trust the state. Slight the good and faithful servant, and promote the unprofitable one from one talent to ten. (Spencer 1853, pp. 271–2)

4

Herbert Spencer's Offspring

It is difficult to overestimate the relevance of Herbert Spencer for his contemporaries. What Spencer did for the Victorians, to quote J. D. Y. Peel, was 'to sum up . . . in an all-embracing synthesis the accumulated knowledge of their age' (Peel 1971, p. 1). But if Herbert Spencer, the system-builder, brought together the 'collected wisdom' of his age, Herbert Spencer the political philosopher was the 'focal point,' in Michael W. Taylor's perceptive definition (Taylor 1996, p. vii), of a larger and growing debate on the limits of state action. His fame went beyond the boundaries of the individualist movement, but his fame was crucial in defining that movement. It is no exaggeration to say that, for years, 'Spencer was the most prominent name to drop when it came to a libertarian vision of unrestricted economic rights' (Doherty 2007, p. 35).

As we have already seen, tragically, Herbert Spencer was fated to witness the *Zeitgeist* – the temper of the age – turn during his own lifetime against what he considered to be the true endpoint of political evolution – namely a freer society. Spencer moved from being the prophet of a promising future to being an embittered guardian of ideas and freedoms rooted in the past. Some one hundred years after *Man Versus the State* was published, F. A. Hayek summarized the alternate fortunes of classical liberalism in history by noting that 'When I was very young, only the very old believed in classical liberalism. Now that I am very old, we're winning a flood of young people to our side' (Blanchard 1984).

Hayek, born in 1899, spent his youth in the dark days of the First World War, fighting in the trenches,[1] when Europe saw the eclipse of an international order of trade and peace that was perhaps the most enduring legacy of the eighteenth century – in this sense, 'a liberal century' indeed. For Spencer, the opposite was true: ideas that were young when he was young somehow 'aged' with him. After the publication of *Man Versus the State*, Spencer reportedly told Andrew Carnegie that 'the wave of opinion carrying us toward Socialism and utter subordination of the individual is becoming irresistible' (quoted in Himmelfarb 1992, p. 309).

In spite of the changing tides of history, Herbert Spencer's political thought was an inspiration for many. In this chapter, we will present some evidence of the influence exercised by Spencer's ideas – ranging from the impact he nevertheless had on 'New Liberals' who couldn't share his political views to the fullest extent to his few true disciples.

A Progeny of Apostates

Political ideas are part of politics: therefore they do not stand alone in this world, but are associated with institutions and organizations. Sometimes, ideas do gravitate around political parties; and the development of party politics and the evolution of political thinking are sometimes intertwined. This certainly happened in the case of British liberalism between the 1880s and the early years of the twentieth century.

On the political side, the Gladstone Cabinet in 1880 was a turning point. Beatrice Webb noted that Gladstone's government 'may be fitly termed a "no man's land" between the old Radicalism and the new Socialism' (Webb 1979, p. 184). The Ground Game Act, the Irish Land Act of 1881 and the Employers' Liability Act defined the legislative framework of a liberalism founded not on the 'method of repeal' dear to Spencer, but rather on the ambition to rectify the evils of the world via legislation.

Moderate individualist G. J. Goschen (1831–1907)[2] noted that 'various economic principles . . . died since 1880 . . . among the most conspicuous casualties let us recall the sad fate of freedom of contract. We seem almost to have arrived at this formula – little freedom in making contracts, much freedom in breaking them' (Goschen 1885, p. 727).

On the intellectual side, the turning point was probably a lecture given in 1881 by Thomas H. Green (1836–82) on liberal legislation and freedom of contract. Green, one of England's foremost philosophers of the nineteenth century, wanted the liberal idea of freedom to go beyond freedom of contract: he defined freedom as 'a positive power of capacity of doing or enjoying something worth doing or enjoying and that, too, something that we do or enjoy with others' (Green 1888, p. 371). The concept of freedom and opportunity were married together. To appropriate the words of one of Green's acolytes, philosopher D. G. Ritchie (1853–1903), 'liberty in the sense of a positive opportunity for self-development is the creation of law and not something that could exist apart from the action of the state' (2002, pp. 139–140).

Green's thought finds fullest expression in his *Lectures on the Principles of Political Obligation* (Green 1986). For Green, the state is a form that society takes in order to uphold rights – but 'rights' are not natural, pre-political rights, but only 'powers' that society allows to individuals to enable them to make a contribution to the common good.

Green presented a justification for the public regulation of the life and property of citizens. Freedom of contract thus could be obliterated, for the sake of allowing people to freely choose among a wider spectrum of opportunities. It has been remarked that 'in the crucial matter of property, Green believed that the duty of the state was to promote its proper use, not to engage directly in its control or ownership' (Barker 1997, p. 22). Nevertheless, Green opened the door for an understanding of liberalism in which state action did not stop when faced by individuals' property.

Followers of 'old' liberalism reunited around the Liberty and Property Defence League, which was founded in 1882 by Lord Elcho, Earl of Wemyss (1818–1914). It took inspiration from Spencer's work, and it was one of a number of similar groups founded to champion the 'classical' liberal tradition that popped up during the last quarter of the nineteenth century. Nevertheless, their combined influence, politically speaking, was negligible compared to that of the emerging forces of New Liberalism, which came to dominate the intellectual scene.

L. T. Hobhouse (1864–1929) and J. A. Hobson (1858–1940) were the most relevant thinkers in this stream of thought. If it is a matter of record that 'one and all of the exponents of New Liberalism' expressed admiration for Spencer (Nisbet 1980, p. 235). Hobson, a freelance writer and economist, was an admirer of Cobden, Mill and Spencer in his youth – but, sharing Spencer's idea of society as ever evolving and progressive, believed that liberalism should itself have a progressive development.[3] Hobson made extensive use of the metaphor of the social organism, but 'for Hobson, unlike Spencer, the image of organism carried with it an articulation of functions in society, functions which could best be supervised and regulated by the state' (Nisbet 1980, p. 301). The social organism metaphor was, according to Freeden (1978, 94–116), crucial indeed for New Liberals.

One thing Hobson clearly retained from his admiration for Spencer was the analysis of imperialism. But pacifism was the only Spencerian *legatum* he really accepted. His theory of imperialism is based on the thesis, later rehashed by Lenin (1870–1924), that imperialism was a direct consequence of the nature of a capitalist economy: when wages were low, industry was faced with a steadily diminishing rate of returns in the home market and so turned to overseas economies (Hobson 1902). Hobson shared a dislike of imperialism, but he did not believe in the natural affinity between capitalism at home and a peaceful foreign policy abroad. Not surprisingly, in a different context, he scorned Auberon Herbert's theory as 'nothing else than a timid form of rich man's anarchism which exploits the philosophic doctrines of monadism for the defence of unsound forms of property' (Hobson 1898).

Hobhouse likewise believed that industrialism needed to be balanced by greater use of the power of the state as a bulwark to shore up the security of each individual. In his *Development and Purpose*, published in 1913, he attempted to blend biological, social and moral progress (à la Spencer) with the idea of economic planning. For Hobhouse, it was the progression of knowledge that finally made it possible to use the state as a facilitator of even more social progress.

In his book *Liberalism*, in particular, he pushed Green's view of freedom further and further. Hobhouse basically ratified the claims of a centralized state, deeming them to be no hindrance to liberty because, for one thing, increasing state control of economic life was actually creating the conditions for enjoying a fuller freedom and, for another, since all social life involved coercion, state coercion was actually preferable to the coercion exercised in society by individuals and groups.

When L. T. Hobhouse's *Liberalism* was published in 1911 (eight years after Spencer's death), a New Liberal government introduced a budget contemplating proposals for progressive taxation, a tax on land, old age pensions, and a scheme of insurance against illness and unemployment. Hobhouse was 'articulating a liberal variant more sympathetic to the activist democratic' (Meadowcroft 1996, p. xix) – and didn't have to wait for some fifty years (as in Dicey's scheme of the interconnections between public opinion and legislation) to find application.

The reader should not be under the impression that New Liberals embraced unqualified socialism. They stressed that their aim was not 'to abolish the competitive system, to socialize all instruments of production, distribution, exchange, and to convert all workers into public employees – but rather to supply all workers at cost with all the economic conditions requisite to the education and employment of their personal powers to their personal advantage and enjoyment' (Hobson 1909, pp. 172–3).

If this tradition of thought, which grew in influence during the twentieth century, was at the same time embodying Spencer's nightmares and showing the signs of his influence, there were many other admirers of Spencer 'on the left,' so to say. The Italian socialist Enrico Ferri (1856–1929) believed that Marxism was the natural culmination of the theories of Darwin (to whom Marx wanted to dedicate *Das Kapital*, an honor Darwin declined) and Spencer. Thorstein Veblen (1857–1929), who tried to criticize capitalism on the basis of an evolutionary progressive rationale, is clearly indebted to Spencer. J. D. Y. Peel reminds us that 'Kropotkin's view of the mechanism of evolution was more Spencerian than Darwinian' (Peel 1971, p. 234).[4]

But criticism did not lack either. The most famous are G. E. Moore (1873–1958) and Henry Sidgwick (1838–1900) who both more or less accused Spencer of committing the naturalist fallacy, pointing out that he claimed that 'better' meant by definition 'more evolved,' whereas 'more evolved' was automatically assumed to be better (Sidgwick 1899).[5]

To the Right of the Father

Spencer's political ideas seem to have aged with the man. From the optimism of *Social Statics* to the bitter pessimism of *Man Versus the State*, some thirty years of developments in legislation and state action intervened. Therefore, it is not surprising that some of Spencer's disciples grew even more suspicious of the nature of the state than he was, radicalizing his message.

If the main aim of classical liberalism has been historically to seize the limits of state action, anarchists of the free-market persuasion took an even more ambitious route.[6]

For anarchists, 'minarchist' libertarians (i.e. supporters of the idea of a minimal state) basically founded their world view on unrealistic bases, since 'given human nature, once the state exists it is impossible to limit its power' (Huerta de Soto 2009, p. 162).

Libertarian anarchism basically builds on a realist attitude towards politics that is typical of classical liberals too. Authors that emphasized how society is split between *tax-payers* and *tax-consumers*, elitist theorists that analyzed political developments as organized minorities always imposing their will on unorganized majorities, public choice economists analyzing the role played by special interest groups in contemporary democracies; they are all attempting to unmask the fictions behind the glowing words of politics. Still, classical liberals believed that the growth of government was a tendency that could somehow be escaped through proper institutional arrangements.

Libertarian anarchists raised the tendency of government power to grow to the status of an iron law of history. They therefore saw any attempt to seize and limit the scope of state action as basically futile. Contrary to Spencer's evolutionary optimism, historical evidence seems to be on the side of libertarian anarchists: our experience of the modern state is by and large the experience of the growth of the modern state.

It is thus perhaps not surprising that libertarian anarchism is a relatively new political doctrine.[7] It entails an awareness of the broken promises of classical liberalism. Its strength lies exactly in the historical failure of the different institutional devices meant to control government's powers (from written constitutions to the separation of powers) – and therefore could hardly be cogent before the mass slaughters of the twentieth century proved the state to be utterly irredeemable.

A sort of inescapable pessimism towards all the attempted means to constrain arbitrary power is matched by the idea that those very services that classical liberals allowed the state to supply in a position of monopoly (arbitration of justice, repression of crime) could be supplied in the marketplace as well. For anarcho-capitalists, the state is not exempt from the natural laws of economics: if consumers of protection services are to receive the best product at the least cost, if innovation is to be allowed to thrive in this field too, then the production of security should be left to the free market. A forebear of anarcho-capitalism,

Gustave de Molinari (1819–1912), wrote in the same year that
Spencer published *Social Statics*, that whenever

> the consumer is not free to buy security wherever he pleases,
> you forthwith see open up a large profession dedicated to
> arbitrariness and bad management. Justice becomes slow and
> costly, the police vexatious, individual liberty is no longer
> respected, the price of security is abusively inflated and ineq-
> uitably apportioned . . . In a word, all the abuses inherent in
> monopoly or in communism crop up. (Molinari 1977)

As all followers of new political doctrines, free market anarchists felt the need to look back, searching for founding fathers
and grandfathers. This process was synthetically narrated by
the very thinker that more than anybody could be credited with
the 'invention' of contemporary free-market anarchism, Murray
Newton Rothbard.[8] In a short article aptly entitled 'Confessions
of a Right-Wing Liberal,' Rothbard reviews the development of
his own political thought, shared in its core principles with a
small *coterie* of young radicals in post-World War II New York. In
planting the seeds of what became the modern libertarian movement, Rothbard recognized that 'all of our political positions,
from the free market in economics to opposing war and militarism, stemmed from our root belief in individual liberty and our
opposition to the state.' In this quest for liberty,

> originally, our historical heroes were such men as Jefferson,
> Paine, Cobden, Bright and Spencer; but as our views
> became purer and more consistent, we eagerly embraced such
> near-anarchists as the voluntarist, Auberon Herbert, and the
> American individualist-anarchists, Lysander Spooner and
> Benjamin R. Tucker. (Rothbard 1968)[9]

Thus, if Spencer is himself a respected figure by libertarian anarchists, Auberon Herbert easily came to mind as the man who
developed 'the Spencerian idea of equal freedom to its logically

consistent anarcho-capitalist end' (Hoppe 2001). To be sure, Herbert claimed he was no anarchist, but his ideas may remind the contemporary reader of the ethos of today's libertarianism: 'There is no choice except between an open market in all things – that is, free acquisition and complete ownership – or a more or less socialistic government' (Herbert 1884, pp. 110–11). His views were derived from Spencer's 'law of equal freedom' – one possible development of which is surely in the direction of anarchy (Gray 1982).

The personal biography of Auberon Herbert is in itself an interesting story. Born in 1838, Herbert was an aristocrat by birth, a typical member of the British upper class. Youngest son of the third Earl of Carnarvon, he went to Eton and Oxford. As a young man, he held commissions in the Army for several years and served briefly with the Seventh Hussars in India (1860). Upon his return to England, he was elected a Fellow of St. John's college in Oxford. He finally entered Parliament as a Liberal in 1872 after having unsuccessfully sought a parliamentary seat both as a Conservative (1865) and as a Liberal (1868).

Herbert's early political career was rather undistinguished as Eric Mack explains:

> During his time in the House of Commons Herbert's most noteworthy political acts were to join Sir Charles Dilke in his declaration of republicanism and to support Joseph Arch's attempts to form an agricultural laborer's union. Although, in hindsight, many of Herbert's actions and words during the sixties and early seventies can be read as harbingers of his later, consistent, libertarianism, he was in reality throughout this period lacking in any consistent set of political principles. (Mack 1978, p. 300)

Auberon Herbert's life and political career changed abruptly after he met Herbert Spencer in 1873. Giving the Herbert Spencer Lecture at Oxford in 1906, Herbert recognized to the fullest extent how deeply he felt indebted 'to Mr. Spencer for his splendid attempt to show us the great meanings that underlie all things – the order, the intelligibility, the coherence, that exist in this world of ours' (Herbert 1906, p. 259).

Herbert thanked Spencer for having 'spoiled my political life.' He explained how:

> I went into the House of Commons, as a young man, believing that we might do much for the people by a bolder and more unsparing use of the powers that belonged to the great law-making machine . . . It was at that moment that I had the privilege of meeting Mr. Spencer, and the talk which we had – a talk that will always remain memorable to me – set me busily to work to study his writings. (Herbert 1906, p. 260)

By reading Spencer, Herbert 'lost faith in the great machine.' More precisely,

> I saw that thinking and acting for others had always hindered, not helped, the real progress; that all forms of compulsion deadened the living forces in a nation; that every evil violently stamped out still persisted, almost always in a worse form, when driven out of sight, and festered under the surface. I no longer believe that the handful of us – however well intentioned we might be – spending our nights in the House, could manufacture the life of a nation, could endow it out of hand with happiness, wisdom and prosperity, and clothe it in all the virtues. (ibidem)

This long passage was worth quoting, for it neatly conveys the main reason why Herbert came to be 'probably the leading English libertarian' (Tame 1980) whose writings came to be widely published and widely discussed. Herbert was a master of rhetoric, endowed with the uncanny skill of seducing his readers by sharing with them his passion and his moral courage.

For Herbert, the experience of meeting Spencer and reading his works was an eye-opener in the sense that it brought him to the understanding that 'no guiding, no limiting or moderating principle existed in the competition of politician against politician.' Spencer conveyed to Herbert an understanding of the shortcomings of democracy. Better to say, what Herbert learnt from Spencer was that a democratic polity was not *per se* more conducive to liberty than any other form of government. Looking to his fellow Commoners from the new perspective that Spencer provided to him, Herbert became aware of a diffuse lust for power lurking behind any plea to the common good, and concluded that corruption was the inescapable by-product of any political system founded on the cornerstone of coercion: 'You cannot serve two masters. You cannot devote yourself to the winning of power, and remain faithful to the great principles. The great principles and the tactics of the political campaign can never be made one, never be reconciled' (Herbert 1906, p. 263).

Eric Mack points out that 'it was even before this intellectual transformation that Herbert had decided, perhaps out of disgust with party politics or uncertainty about his own convictions, not to stand for re-election in 1874' (Mack 1978, p. 300). This newly acquired distaste for the Parliament and its ways, however, did not prompt Herbert to renounce all political engagement altogether.

On the contrary, Herbert never abandoned a deep engagement in the political fight: in due course he merely adjusted the means he was using in order for them to be fully compatible with his own political goals. Before abandoning altogether the prospect of using parliamentary politics to advance the cause of liberty, in 1879 he sought Liberal support to regain a seat in Nottingham. 'At that point,' Mack writes, 'his uncompromising individualist radicalism was not acceptable to the majority of the Central Council of the Liberal Union of Nottingham.' Later on, he even tried to establish a new party, called the Party of Individual Liberty.

Herbert was extensively engaged in anti-militaristic efforts, in rallies against jingoism and against war on Russia in the 1870s, the intervention in Egypt in the early 1880s and, later on, the Second Anglo-Boer War, and in publishing efforts conceived to spread the ideas of liberty. He founded the magazine *Free Life*, writing at the same time for such leading contemporary journals as N*ineteenth Century*, *Fortnightly Review*, *Contemporary Review* and *The Humanitarian*. During the 1890s, Herbert engaged in published exchanges with prominent New Liberals and socialists of his day such as J. A. Hobson. He even came to participate in the debate around *Liberty* magazine, edited by the American individualist anarchist Benjamin Tucker (1854–1939) who, on the occasion of Herbert's death, came to celebrate him as 'a true anarchist in everything but name. How much better (and how much rarer) to be an anarchist in everything but name than to be an anarchist in name only!' (Watner 1986).[10]

In all these efforts, Herbert always considered himself to be on the fringe of the contemporary liberal movement, occupying somehow the extreme left wing of the individualist camp, the one which was most willing to carry liberty to the fullest extent. He remained loyal to a Lockean version of natural rights theory, by which every human being holds a right to her own person, her mind and body, and therefore to her labour and to the fruits of her own labour. 'The creed of rights,' he wrote, 'leads as certainly to the elevation of the human race as the creed of socialism, founded on force, leads to the degradation of it' (Herbert 1884, p. 106). The law of equal liberty, the idea that since each person has these rights, and that everybody is under a moral obligation to respect these rights in everybody else, was the core of Herbert's thinking.

Herbert championed the 'system of the widest possible liberty' in which 'each man thinks and acts according to his own judgment and his own sense of right.' A system in which any man is 'be it for good or evil, the owner and possessor of his own self, and he has to bear the responsibility of that ownership and possession to the full' (Herbert 1885, pp. 124–5).

Auberon Herbert was able to frame his views in a purely Spencerian fashion. He made the positive case for liberty building on the natural rights lexicon of the Spencer of *Social Statics*, but condemned statism by using arguments from Spencerian evolutionism. He wrote that

> all infringements of liberty sin in a twofold way. They tend to uniformity by excluding natural variety, and they give external protection at the costs of preventing the development of self-protection, saving the pain of the present by doubling it in the future. (Herbert 1884, p. 109)

Herbert came to be so popular among modern libertarians because he was clearly among the first to realize how this doctrine could hardly be reconciled with allowing governments to monopolize the use of force in society. Herbert's writings are by and large directed against the very idea that there could be something like a legitimate use of force in society. In an 1894 essay, stupendously entitled 'The Ethics of Dynamite,' Herbert came to write that since

> undeniably the great purpose of government is the compulsion of A by B and C to do what he does not want to do . . . dynamite is not opposed to government; it is, on the contrary, government in its most intensified and concentrated form. (Herbert 1894, p. 192)

Herbert's notion of voluntary taxation was under many respects built on Spencer's 'right to ignore the state' (as highlighted by Rothbard 1970, p. 165), but did not encounter much fortune among following writers. Rothbard highlighted the proposal's inconsistency. Herbert's idea had two different problems. If the voluntarily financed government did permit competition in defense provision, 'there would soon no longer be a central government over the territory.' Therefore, the voluntarily paid tax would simply become a *price*, the price charged by one defense agency among others. But in the case that the voluntarily financed government would monopolize the supply of defense and justice services, the system would show an 'unstable equilibrium': the fee charged will not be 'neutral' but a sort of 'compulsory membership,' and moreover it will most probably not last as 'voluntary' very long (Rothbard 1970, pp. 165–7).

The other Spencer disciple who tried to move 'to the right of the father' was Wordsworth Donisthorpe (1847–1914). Donisthorpe parted company with the Liberty and Property Defence League in 1888 over what he considered to be the excessive moderation of the league. A barrister, Donisthorpe wrote extensively and did not hide his association with the anarchist camp. In a lecture he gave to the Fabian Society, reprinted under the title 'A word for anarchy,' he sided with democracy as 'not the government of many as opposed to the government of the few, but the government of all.' He expected 'some good from democracy. And what is that good? Why nothing more or less than our liberty. We support democracy because it leads straight to anarchy' (Donisthorpe 1894, pp. 254, 257).

Donisthorpe admired Spencer and used his ideas, but not without a few disagreements. He rejected Spencer's adherence to the individual rights paradigm, providing his own interpretation of the social organism analogy as a philosophical scheme conductive – paradoxically – to the freedom of the component parts. He preferred 'to regard my rights not as legacy from a great mind, but as liberties which I exercise through the restraints which society in its wisdom places on the liberties of others' (Donisthorpe 1894, p. 391), but he was firmly convinced that 'the whole history of civilization is the history of a struggle to establish a relation between society and its units, between the whole and its party, which is neither absolute socialism or absolute anarchy; but a state in which, by action and reaction of each upon each, such an adaptation shall take place, that the welfare of the whole is and that of the units shall eventually become coincident and not antagonistic.' The problem of civilization, the development of the social organism was 'integration without impairing the individuality of the component units' (1894, p. 303). The final stage, though probably unreachable, was anarchy.

Donisthorpe's political proposals were extreme. He advocated the virtually completed withdrawal of legislation to reach a status of perfect law compatible with perfect freedom. He was a proto-feminist, intolerant towards the state regulation of marriage and families, and campaigned for the 'private' and the 'local.' Moreover, his idea of local government was that 'the highest form of local government is one of complete and unqualified free enterprise' (Donisthorpe 1894, p. 26).

Born in America

In public discourse, Spencer is often associated with so-called social Darwinism. Since arguably 'Darwin was not an original social thinker' (Paul 2009, p. 240), the label of social Darwinism is usually understood to refer – more or less consciously – to a vague image of extreme free-market individualism, and to ideas that are likewise commonly associated with Spencer. As it was remarked, one reason why, in spite of the many qualifications about the rationale of his evolutionism, Spencer is still by and large considered a social Darwinist lies in 'his worldwide popularity and influence' (Hawkins 2003, p. 98).

The social Darwinist label was popularized by American historian Richard Hofstadter (1916–70) in a path-breaking and much cited work. A New Deal liberal,[11] Hofstadter saw social Darwinism as a conservative ideology that appropriated the theory of evolution by natural selection to support an unrestricted laissez-faire. If Herbert Spencer was seen as the father of such an ideology, then William Graham Sumner was his most eminent scion.

William Graham Sumner was born in New Jersey in 1840, the son of an English immigrant. He grew up in Hartford, Connecticut, and attended Yale University. Intending to become a minister, Sumner went abroad for training; he traveled throughout Europe learning French, Greek and Hebrew. He studied theology at Oxford. Upon returning to the United

States, he took a job at his alma mater and, in July 1869, he was ordained a priest in the Protestant Episcopal Church.

A very successful teacher at Yale, Sumner was a hard man, sticking to his principles no matter what, unabashed in generating controversy. He was not a believer in natural law, and attacked the very idea of natural rights, believing they could be used to pretend that anybody had a natural right to society providing him a living. He was a sociologist whose most famous and lasting work was his 1906 *Folkways*, which explained the emergence of rights and political institutions from the fabric of society. For Sumner, rights were nothing more than folkways crystallized in law. *Mores* were sovereign over political speculation. Especially in later years, he was increasingly lenient towards moral relativism.

Sumner's name is associated with a *cliché* of social Darwinism. In his exposition, he epitomizes the popular conception that, if we reject the principle of the survival of the fittest, we must be prepared to accept that of the survival of the least fit. 'The former carries society forward and favors its best members; the latter carries society downward and favors all its worst members' (Sumner 1914, p. 25).

For him, the survival of the fittest was to be seen in action when population growth puts pressure on resource. Progress has meaning only in relation to 'the laws of population and the diminishing return, in their combination, are the iron spur which had driven the race on to all which it has ever achieved' (Sumner 1881, p. 175–6).

As compared to Spencer, Sumner 'eschewed optimism' and was less confident in the inevitability of progress (Hawkins 2003, p. 109). But in Sumner's political thought, and not infrequently in the uncompromising directness of some of his statements in favour of natural selection or against public aid, his Protestantism often comes back to the surface. As it was noted, his success as an intellectual was precisely due to the fact that 'he provided his age with a synthesis of three great products of Western capitalist culture: the Protestant ethic, the doctrines

126 *Herbert Spencer*

of classical economics, and . . . natural selection' (Hofstadter 1992, p. 51). Coming close to be a living proof of Max Weber's ruminations on Puritan ethics and the spirit of capitalism, Sumner saw in economic success the inevitable product of thrift and diligence.

He understood the ratio of land to population as the key fact in founding society: the ultimate source of men's wealth is the soil, and therefore everything in their existence is ultimately determined by a struggle for existence in which scarcity of soil is the determinant factor. When men are few and land is abundant (or, which is the same, progress enables them to make more of less land), the struggle for existence is less tough and representative government can emerge. When population presses upon the land supply, hunger arises and militancy flourishes.

In this view, the struggle of man over nature is a constant of history, and capitalism is conducive at keeping up 'a combined assault of Nature for the means of subsistence.' For Sumner, capitalism is far from nature: it is one of the great products of modern civilization.

We can say Sumner saw modern capitalism in a Spencerian vein. For him

> the modern industrial system is a great social cooperation. It is automatic and instinctive in its operation. The adjustment of organs takes place naturally. The parties are held together by impersonal forces: supply and demand. They may never see each other; they may be separated by half the circumference of the globe. Their cooperation in the social effort is combined and distributed again by financial machinery, and the rights and interests are measured and satisfied without any special treaty or convention at all. All this goes on so smoothly and naturally that we forget to notice it. (Sumner 2007, p. 40)

In his 1883 *What Social Classes Owe to Each Other,* Sumner attacked social envy on the grounds that 'the aggregation of large fortunes is not at all a thing to be regretted. On the contrary, it

is a necessary conditions of many forms of social advance'
(Sumner 2007, p. 34). What was dangerous for society, was not
the formation of a class of wealthy or even super-wealthy people,
it was 'the waste of capital' chiefly due 'to ignorance and bad
management, especially to state control of public works.'

In the same essay, he deconstructs a holistic view of the state.

> During the last ten years I have read a great many books and
> articles, especially by German writers, in which an attempt has
> been made to set up 'the state' as an entity having conscience,
> power, and will sublimated above human limitations, and as
> constituting a tutelary genius over us all. I have never been
> able to find in history or experience anything to fit this con-
> cept . . . My notion of the state has dwindled with growing
> experience of life. As an abstraction, the state is to me only all
> of us. In practice – that is, when it exercises will or adopts a
> line of action, it is only a little group of men chosen in a very
> haphazard way by the majority of us to perform certain ser-
> vices for all of us. (Sumner 2007, p. 22)

Sumner spent all of his life fighting against tariffs, seeing protectionism as 'fallacious, absurd, and impracticable' (Sumner
1888, p. 156). Protectionism was the 'ism which teaches that
waste makes wealth,' and was understood by Sumner as a *political*
phenomenon. He highlighted that 'the protective system is a
domestic system, for domestic purposes, and it is sought by
domestic means. The one who pays, and the one who gets, are
both Americans. The victim and the beneficiary are amongst our-
selves' (Sumner 1886, p. 123). Tariffs were the means by which
some groups gained a price above the natural market level, and
therefore a rent to be paid by all the other national taxpayers.

Sumner's other foe, together with protectionism, was war. His
analysis was in this sense truly analogous to Spencer's:

> We see that militancy and peacefulness have existed side by
> side in human society from the beginning just as they exist now.

A peaceful society must be industrial because it must produce instead of plundering; it is for this reason that the industrial type of society is the opposite of the militant type. In any state on the continent of Europe today these two types of societal organization may be seen interwoven with each other and fighting each other. Industrialism builds up; militancy wastes. (Sumner 1903, p. 28)

But Sumner had an understanding of how wars and crises can produce an enlargement of state functions that was even more profound than Spencer's, perhaps because he could observe the real world experiment conducted upon the United States after the Civil War. He feared 'the conquest of the United States by Spain,' by which he meant the substantial transformation of the United States into a European modern state, motivated by the greed of conquest and imperial vanity.

Sumner understood the circumstances of the United States as quite exceptional. He 'inherited classical liberalism as a tradition cherishing account of the historically exceptional "civil liberty" of America' (Adcock 2009, p. 33). Of course, the land was abundant for a small population, and therefore the difficulties of the struggle with nature were alleviated. But furthermore, 'this country owes its existence to a revolt against the colonial and navigation system which, as I have said, Spain first put in practice. The English colonial system never was even approximately so harsh and tyrannical as that of Spain' (Sumner 1898, p. 315). He further added that

my patriotism is of the kind which is outraged by the notion that the United States never was a great nation until in a petty three months' campaign it knocked to pieces a poor, decrepit, bankrupt old state like Spain. To hold such an opinion as that is to abandon all American standards, to put shame and scorn on all that our ancestors tried to build up here, and to go over to the standards of which Spain is a representative. (Sumner 1898, p. 344)

In this passage, Sumner displays the affection for modesty in government and symbols that pervades all his works. Not only did he crusade against war and protectionism, but he also fought plutocracy, which he saw emerging from a market system corrupted by protectionism and state interference. In all his works, the hero he wanted to vindicate was 'the forgotten man':

> the simple, honest laborer, ready to earn his living by productive work. We pass him by because he is independent, self-supporting, and asks no favors. He does not appeal to the emotions or excite the sentiments. He only wants to make a contract and fulfill it, with respect on both sides and favor on neither side. (Sumner 1883, p. 476)

The forgotten man, the middle-class taxpayer was 'the real victim' of the machinations of 'philanthropists and humanitarians,' of the expansion of state power, of state 'benevolence,' of the *grandeur* of expansionist policies.

This distaste for grandeur is constant in Sumner's writings. This helps us to understand why, as he was active and interested in the politics of his times, he was deeply suspicious of social engineering. 'Social improvement is not to be won by direct effort. It is secondary, and results from physical or economic improvements,' he wrote, adding that

> that is the reason why schemes of direct social amelioration always have an arbitrary, sentimental, and artificial character, while true social advance must be a product and a growth . . . An improvement in surgical instruments or in anæsthetics really does more for those who are not well off than all the declamations of the orators and pious wishes of the reformers. Civil service reform would be a greater gain to the laborers than innumerable factory acts and eight-hour laws. Free trade would be a greater blessing to 'the poor man' than all the devices of all the friends of humanity if they could be realized. If the economists could satisfactorily solve the problem of the

regulation of paper currency, they would do more for the wages class than could be accomplished by all the artificial doctrines about wages which they seem to feel bound to encourage. If we could get firm and good laws passed for the management of savings banks, and then refrain from the amendments by which those laws are gradually broken down, we should do more for the non-capitalist class than by volumes of laws against corporations and the excessive power of capital. (Sumner 2007, p. 87)

Unfettered competition – free markets – are more conducive to social evolution than any alternative:

Instead of endeavoring to redistribute the acquisitions which have been made between the existing classes, our aim should be to increase, multiply, and extend the chances. Such is the work of civilization. Every old error or abuse which is removed opens new chances of development to all the new energy of society. Every improvement in education, science, art, or government expands the chances of man on earth. Such expansion is no guarantee of equality. On the contrary, if there be liberty, some will profit by the chances eagerly and some will neglect them altogether. Therefore, the greater the chances the more unequal will be the fortune of these two sets of men. So it ought to be, in all justice and right reason . . . But if we can expand the chances we can count on a general and steady growth of civilization and advancement of society by and through its best members. In the prosecution of these chances we all owe to each other good-will, mutual respect, and mutual guarantees of liberty and security. Beyond this nothing can be affirmed as a duty of one group to another in a free state. (Sumner 2007, p. 88)

For his critics, Sumner 'has come to exemplify the ruthless advocacy of the survival of the fittest with a concomitant disregard for the impact of the struggle for existence on the losers' (Hawkins 2003, p. 115). However, even Richard Hofstadter could show some sort of sympathy for Sumner. To critics accusing him of being an intellectual prostitute for capitalism, Hofstadter replied that they

> showed little comprehension of Sumner's character or the governing motives of his mind. He was doctrinaire because his ideas were bred in his bone. He was not a business hireling, nor did he feel himself to be the spokesman of plutocracy, but rather of the middle class. (Hofstadter 1992, p. 63)

Sumner should be considered a model of consistency, like Spencer, in the sense that he was convinced that the doctrine of *laissez-faire* is just as applicable to society as it is to the economy. The moralist Sumner feared paternal government because 'men who are taught to expect government inspectors to come and take care of them lose all their education in liberty' (Sumner 2007, p. 56). On the contrary, 'society . . . does not need any care or supervision. Society needs first of all to be freed from these meddlers – that is, to be let alone.' He was one genuine champion of laissez-faire. 'Let us translate it into blunt English, and it will read: Mind your own business . . . It is nothing but the doctrine of liberty' (Sumner 2007, p. 67).

Notes

[1] The impact that fighting as a soldier in the First World War at age 19 had on the development of the thought of Hayek can hardly be overstated. For one thing, the war left him deaf in his left ear and weakened by malaria. But, first and foremost, he saw the political ideal of a multinational, multiracial and culturally diverse Europe (that was embodied – however imperfectly – in the Habsburg Empire) disintegrating beyond his very eyes.

[2] On Goschen, see Spinner (1973).

[3] Alas, 'Hobson employed the analogy of a natural organism to describe society and its political function . . . in a manner similar to that used by T. H. Huxley and unlike that used by individualists such as Spencer' (Barker 1997, p. 31).

[4] Peel also highlights how in his *Mutual Aid*, 'Prince Peter Kropotkin, pacifist and anarchist, though his social ideas differed markedly from Spencer's, only quoted Spencer in support of his own views. There are passages in *Mutual Aid* which would not have been out of place in *Social Statics*' (Peel 1971, p. 147).

[5] The examination of Spencer's criticisms on the part of two giants of the history of philosophy goes beyond the scope of this short monograph. For a forceful rebuttal of Moore, see Gray (1982).

[6] Free-market anarchists typically refer to themselves as 'libertarian,' but the use of this word is indeed ambiguous, since in the contemporary political discourse 'libertarianism' is more often than not associated with a political doctrine associated with the radical limitation of the state, rather than its extinction. Among the contemporary political philosophers, the greatest champion of libertarianism is considered to be Robert Nozick who, in his *Anarchy, State, and Utopia* (1974), developed perhaps the most stringent case for a minimal state vis-à-vis the welfare state but anarchy too. Still, contemporary libertarian anarchism developed up to a certain extent in a critical reaction to Nozick's work. See Barnett (1977), Childs (1977) and Rothbard (1977).

[7] There are of course examples of progenitors besides the very same Auberon Herbert (e.g. Gustave de Molinari [1977]).

[8] Rothbard was a voracious reader and a bulimically prolific writer, giving considerable contributions in fields as different as political theory, economic theory, and the history of economic thought. But he was also a tireless political and cultural activist whose life-long dream was to develop a successful anti-statist movement in the United States. Rothbard forged 'anarcho-capitalism' (as he called it) by merging together the economic theory of the so-called 'Austrian school of economics,' with the Lockean natural rights tradition, plus a distinctive and original belief that they both should bring to the complete rebuttal of the institutions of the state.

[9] Ronald Hamowy described in a similar way the pantheon of the American 'Old Right' in a polemic with William F. Buckley (1925–2008) over the influence exerted by the *National Review*, the magazine founded and edited by Buckley on the US right-wing movement. 'At a time when the Left had a virtual monopoly on all intellectual activity,' Hamowy explained, 'during the early 40s, a small but ever-growing libertarian movement began to emerge. Its leaders were such eminent publicists and political thinkers as Isabel Paterson, Rose Wilder Lane, Garet Garrett, Albert Jay Nock, and Frank Chodorov. Philosophically, it was firmly dedicated to individual liberty, and

consequently embraced free enterprise in economics, a strict adherence to the civil liberties of the individual, and peace. Historically, it ranked among its heroes Jefferson, Tom Paine, Thoreau, and Herbert Spencer' (Hamowy and Buckley 1961, p. 3).

[10] Tucker announced Herbert's death in this way. For the comprehensive indexes of *Liberty* heroically compiled by Wendy McElroy, see: http://tmh.floonet.net/articles/ind_intr.html .

[11] Speaking of the work to which the label 'social Darwinism' owes most of its fame, David S. Brown has aptly noted that Hoftstadter's book *Social Darwinisim in American Thought 1860–1915* 'is a product of the 1930 struggle to carve out a new liberal tradition' (Brown 2006, p. 28).

Who Should Read Spencer Today?

A philosopher for the Victorian age, Herbert Spencer was forgotten – if not altogether reviled – for most of the twentieth century. His thought was often oversimplified and reduced to a mere caricature. His evolutionism was dismissed as teleological and naive, in spite of the growing support for evolutionary theory at large. In the twentieth century, his individualism looked outdated and out of place. New Liberals and socialists were uncomfortable with it because of its economic policy. Conservatives may well be embarrassed by Spencer's uncompromising anti-imperialism, for his distaste of *grandeur* in matters of state. Michael Taylor observed that

> perhaps the most important reason for Spencer's neglect, however, is the fact that for most of his mature years he was engaged in elaborating a defence of a social and economic order which was already in the process of passing away. (Taylor 1992, p. viii)

As a theorist of laissez-faire, Spencer was buried with the very principles he upheld. As noted by J. W. Burrow (1966, p. 180), his name has become a 'period label' precisely because his influence faded away.

In this respect, the difference between Spencer and the many other forgotten individualists relates basically to the fact that, contrary to them, Spencer was well read and well known during his lifetime. He was renowned and appreciated as a philosopher, recognized by the public as one of the leading interpreters of the *Zeitgeist*, a protagonist in the debates of his age as a leading public intellectual.

This does not imply that Spencer did not have intellectual adversaries and critics over his lifetime. It has been often pointed out that both Darwin and Mill, even though they praised him in public, in their private correspondence showed a considerable scepticism about the real, scientific value of the *Synthetic Philosophy*. Politeness was held in very different consideration in the nineteenth century, for sure. But it is impossible to overlook the fact that Spencer engaged the major thinkers of his age and his country, and was himself considered as such.

Synthetic Philosophy may have come to be disregarded by history for a variety of reasons. The notion that the breadth of thought of a single author can encompasses so many different realms, from biology to psychology to politics, has been discredited. Intellectuals are now highly specialized professionals, and the thinker who dares conceive an all-encompassing system is more often than not seen as a dilettante.

What interests us, here, is the fate of Spencer's political tenets. It is true that supporters of limited government went out of fashion with the ever-growing rise of government. For most of the last century, the conventional wisdom has dictated an increase in state functions; the kind of attitude that Spencer so forcefully portrayed and attacked in 'Overlegislation' worked at full speed for decades. Spencer's evolutionary rationale for a free society was particularly unbearable for those preaching an ever greater involvement of government in healing or preventing social ills. *Laissez-faire l'évolution* was laissez-faire indeed. Not surprisingly, no less than a figure than John Maynard Keynes (1883–1946) pointed out that laissez-faire was akin to the Darwinian theory. 'The principle of the survival of the fittest could be regarded as a vast generalization of the Ricardian economics' (Keynes 1972, p. 276).

Of course, that Keynes was unlikely to love Spencer is something the reader of this book could have guessed just by reading its table of contents. It has been observed that 'Spencer is neglected because his conservative individualistic politics are disliked on a normative level, not because he extrapolated political implications from his theories,' but he is often no less neglected by his 'ideological friends' than by his 'ideological foes' (Roark 2004, p. 3). What is actually more surprising, and interesting, is how the intellectual adversaries of Keynes have by and large ignored Spencer.

It is true, as we already mentioned, that the American libertarian movement, both in its minimal state guise and in its anarchist wing, came to consider Herbert Spencer as a hero of its cause. Albert J. Nock made explicit and frequent reference to Spencer (Nock 1935). When, in 1965, Chicago economist Yale Brozen (1918–98) came to write on 'The Revival of Traditional Liberalism,' he opened his work with a quotation from 'Overlegislation.' Tibor Machan, echoing Albert J. Nock, wrote that 'what Spencer did for libertarianism is what Marx did for communism – provide it with what was to be a full-blown scientific justification' (Machan 1978, p. 9). But whereas communists are Marxists, libertarians – including the author of those lines, Tibor Machan – are not Spencerians.

It is a fact that the greatest champions of market economics in the twentieth century were not particularly well acquainted with Spencer's works. For one thing, a renewed scholarly interest in Spencer did not appear until the 1970s. Heralded by Burrow (1966), this revival was led by Andreski (1972) and Peel (1971). The authors elucidated the value of Spencer's anticipatory works in sociology, and contributed substantially to a growing body of scholarship assessing the impact of Spencer in social sciences in a much fairer way than in the immediate past.

The influence exercised by Spencer on Durkheim and Parsons was crucial, in this process, as it led a newer generation of sociologists to go beyond the customary dismissal of social Darwinism and assess the true legacy of Spencer. Peel (1971) also investigated Spencer's politics, highlighting its roots in Cobdenism.

From then on, historians made important contributions, and Spencer came to be a scholarly interest – however minor – of distinguished political thinkers such as John Gray (1982) and Hillel Steiner (1982). The 1982 issue of *History of Political Thought*, which includes their contributions, is a landmark in contemporary Spencerian scholarship.

Some of those articles resulted from a Liberty Fund symposium organized in 1979, in which eleven scholars confronted themselves with the thought of Herbert Spencer. The proceedings, published in different outlets, paved the way for subsequent scholars: Spencer was now seen as a perfectly legitimate and respectable scholarly interest, and papers on him regularly – if not frequently – appear in scholarly journals.

Wiltshire (1978), Turner (1985), Weinstein (1998), Gray (1996) and Taylor (1992) provide the contemporary reader with a rich menu of different possible interpretations of Spencerianism. The depth and seriousness of their work is evidence of the importance and intellectual weight of the object of this book, but what none of them provides is a *libertarian* account of Spencer. Francis (2007), certainly the most ambitious of the works on Spencer published after Peel (1971), goes as far as to argue against the usual enrolment of Spencer into the ranks of sympathizers of market freedom and free enterprise. If Spencer was really the Marx of libertarians, why then they did neglect him so badly?

Spencerian Themes for the Twentieth Century

The main reason why libertarians could forget Spencer and live happy ever after was that some of the most relevant Spencerian themes were at the center of the theoretical work of a giant of classical liberalism and social sciences in the twentieth century: Friedrich A. von Hayek.

Hayek is the leading champion of an evolutionary classical liberalism in the last century, and his ideas are indeed, as Andrew

Gamble puts it, 'close in some respects to those of Herbert Spencer.' For Gamble,

> there is an important difference. Spencer thought it was possible to identify evolutionary laws, and on this basis argued that the final destination of human societies, their highest stage of development, was laissez-faire. Hayek shared his goal . . . but disagreed that it was inevitable. For him, no single destination lay at the end of contemporary social development.' (Gamble 1996, p. 181)

In contrast, Nisbet saw Hayek as akin to Spencer in that the latter was too 'a strong voice among our continuing prophets of progress' (Nisbet 1980, p. 299).

Hayek may have resented such a characterization, being a strong critic of theories that wanted to impose political progress through social engineering efforts; but his vision of the evolution of society can nevertheless be read under an optimistic, and progressive, light.

There is no evidence that Hayek ever had a deep knowledge of Herbert Spencer's works (there is no evidence he had but a vague recognition of his name), but they can be considered as part of the same political camp, as well as part of the very same research programme. For John Gray, indeed, they are united by the same 'aspiration of embedding the defence of liberty in a broad evolutionary framework' (Gray 1998, p. 103).

If the lack of any 'teleological' ethos in Hayek, as understood by Gamble, contributes to differentiate his evolutionism from Spencer's, we can nonetheless easily discern common ground in other areas. In particular, two themes can be seen as basically common between the two.

First, as we saw, Spencer's evolutionism builds upon a synthesis of natural selection and direct adaptation. A strong emphasis on learning, on the part of individuals and groups of individuals, can actually bring us to see him and Hayek as closer under this respect. For both of them, evolution is a continuous striving and learning.

Secondly, although Hayek did not imagine a free society as the end of the path of human evolution, his idea of evolution is coloured by the notion of increasing complexity as a feature of evolution itself. The path is from the simple to the complex. And this, speaking of social orders and not of natural organisms, brings us from face-to-face societies to complex societies, from simple schemes of interaction to intricate markets composed of a plurality of players – a Spencerian theme indeed.

On the first point, Hayek spoke of the 'twin ideas of evolution and spontaneous order' (Hayek 1967, p. 77). To understand what he meant we have to think about 'the use of knowledge in society,' which is by and large the main theme of Hayek's work. The key problem of all human action is the problem of how to secure the subjectively best use of dispersed resources, known to some particular members of society but not available in its totality, even in principle, to any single individual (or central authority).

The world around us is for Hayek 'conjectural' in the sense that it is informed by a pre-existing system of classification in light of which events are interpreted. Such a system is the combined product of cultural evolution and individual learning. The whole process of learning (i.e. the process by which knowledge grows) can be seen as a procedure that allows for correcting, adjusting and refining conjectural knowledge in the light of the currently available knowledge brought by experience. This is a point seriously intertwined with Hayek's exploration of the human mind, contained in one of his most ambitious – and complex – works, *The Sensory Order* (Hayek 1952). Of course it cannot be an object of analysis of the present book, but it is worth recalling that Spencer himself invested a lot in his own theory of the functioning of the mind, which was exposed in the *Principles of Psychology*. For Spencer, the mind was composed of 'feelings' (portions of consciousness), each of them being in its turn a compound of a number of nervous shocks. The consolidation of 'units of feeling' forms sensations, which in turn are consolidated in knowledge of sensations to form the smallest separable portion of what we can call thought (Spencer 1855). The formation of the mind was in fact a compounding and recompounding of primitive sensations into higher states of consciousness, which obeyed the general law of evolution by the fact it exhibited the same features of integration and differentiation. This was the grounding of Spencer's evolutionary theory – since this process resulted in features of the physical nervous structures that could be hereditarily transmitted.[1]

In *The Constitution of Liberty*, Hayek notes how a selection process operates on the various kinds of knowledge: all of them are 'adaptations to past experience which have grown up by selective elimination of less suitable conduct' (Hayek 1960, p. 26). For Hayek, the advance of civilization does not depend on humans being omniscient and results in a quest from simplicity to complexity.

As he puts it in his ground-breaking 1945 essay, 'The Use of Knowledge in Society':

> As Alfred Whitehead has said in another connection, 'It is a profoundly erroneous truism, repeated by all copy books and by eminent people when they are making speeches, that we should cultivate the habit of thinking what we are doing. The precise opposite is the case. Civilization advances by extending the number of important operations which we can perform without thinking about them.' This is of profound significance in the social field. We make constant use of formulas, symbols, and rules whose meaning we do not understand and through the use of which we avail ourselves of the assistance of knowledge which individually we do not possess. We have developed these practices and institutions by building upon habits and institutions which have proved successful in their own sphere and which have in turn become the foundation of the civilization we have built up. (Hayek 1945, p. 528)

This was particularly true for the price system which for Hayek was 'just one of those formations which man has learned to use (though he is still very far from having learned to make the best use of it) after he had stumbled upon it without understanding it' (Hayek 1945).

In *The Constitution of Liberty*, Hayek builds on the concept, explaining that the developments in civilization rest upon accidents happening: accidents in the way that knowledge and attitudes, skills and habits, get combined. These accidents (these mutations) are a source of random variation: they therefore allow new ways of doing things to be tried.

A similar process can be observed with the cultural evolution of groups in society:

> which individuals and which groups succeed and continue to exist depends as much on the goals that they pursue, the values that govern their action, as on the tools and capacities at their command. Whether a group will prosper or be extinguished depends as much on the ethical code it obeys, or the ideals of beauty or well-being that guide it, as on the degree to which it has learned or not learned to satisfy its material needs. (Hayek 1960a, p. 36)

As remarked by Gamble, Hayek maintained that it is far from certain that 'the new state [brought back by evolution] will give us more satisfaction than the old' (Hayek 1960b, p. 41).

In *Law, Legislation and Liberty*, Hayek clearly distinguished between 'spontaneous orders' and 'organizations' on the key variable of their respective complexity. The former are self-generating orders, what the Greeks called *kosmos*. The latter are artificial orders, deliberately constructed as such and what the Greeks called *taxis*. Constructed orders are relatively simple; they are based on concrete relations, and they aim at accomplishing specific purposes. A spontaneously grown order can, instead, be extremely complex, it is typically based on abstract relations, and it cannot be said to serve a specific purpose. Agents in organizations are led by specific commands; those in spontaneous orders are bound by abstract rules.[2]

This is exactly the same argument used by Spencer in distinguishing among industrialism and militancy. Industrialism needs only the possibility of achieving enforcement for contracts – militancy needs deliberately constructed plans. One is a self-generating order; the other is a constructed order.

As we saw, Spencer held dear to himself the notion of spontaneous order:

> The worldwide transactions conducted in merchant's offices, the rush of traffic filling our streets, the retail distributing system which brings everything in easy reach and delivers the necessaries of daily life to our door, are not of government origin. All these are the results of the spontaneous activities of citizens, separated or grouped. Nay, to these spontaneous activities governments owe the very means of performing their duties. Divest the political machinery of all the aids which science and art have yielded it – leave it those only which state officials have invented; and its functions would cease. The very language in which its laws are registered and the orders of its agents daily given, is an instrument not in the remotest degree due to the legislator; but one which had unawares grown up during men's intercourse while pursuing their personal satisfactions. (Spencer 1981, pp. 134–5)

Hayek's own strongest arguments against the notion of social justice, and by and large socialism, resemble Spencer's own arguments. The ever-increasing complexity brought by evolution cannot be moulded by planners and social engineers: the fundamental error of planners and statists of all kinds is the attempt to apply to the whole of society concepts that are only relevant within the boundaries of an organization. The fundamental error of the constructivists is to think that the commands used to accomplish goals within an organization can be used to accomplish social ends within 'that spontaneous order which Adam Smith called "the Great Society" and Sir Karl Popper

called "the Open Society'" (Hayek 1973, p. 2). And, we may add,
Herbert Spencer called 'industrialism.'

Hayek built on Adam Smith and the other authors he recognized as the core group of the Scottish enlightenment thinkers:

> For the first time it was shown that an evident order which
> was not the product of a designing human intelligence need
> not therefore to be ascribed to the design of a higher super-
> natural intelligence, but there was a third possibility – the
> emergence of order as the result of adaptive evolution. (Hayek
> 1960, p. 59)

As Ronald Hamowy later put it, 'perhaps the greatest sociological contribution made by that group of writers whom we
today regard as constituting the Scottish enlightenment is the
notion of spontaneously generated social orders' (Hamowy
1987, p.3).

For Hayek, in very much the same way we 'stumbled upon' the
price system, so human society is largely governed by 'a tradition
of rules of conduct, existing apart from any one individual who
had learnt them.' Social order is not the outcome of the workings of human reason – it is rather the opposite which is closer
to the truth:

> It was when these learnt rules, involving classifications of
> different kinds of objects, began to include a sort of model
> of the environment that enabled man to predict and antici-
> pate in action external events, that what we called reason
> appeared. There was then probably much more 'intelligence'
> incorporated in the system of rule of conduct than in man's
> thoughts about his surroundings. (Hayek 1979, p. 157)

In a very well-known formulation, for Hayek not only the price
system, but human society at large, is the product of human
action but not of human design. It emerges from human actions

because individuals cooperate with each other without compulsion, and even without the impulse provided by a social contract or any idea of forming a whole society. Forms of cooperation are fluid and varied but the continuous interactions among social actors bring about a society which, in taking shape, develops institutions and rules that subsequently becomes its distinguishing marks.

There is a strong parallel between a social order at large and the free market system. In a market men cooperate with each other because by doing so they see opportunities for an easier, surer or greater attainment of their ends. But no individual ever needs to see the full extent of the market, nor needs to be conscious of being an element of what appears to be a market. When we consider markets, we look at something which arises from human choices in action and which cannot be understood without seeing how the various choices interact, but in which no single choice is purposefully and deliberately directed at the formation of the whole market. In due course, all markets develop rules – as do all societies.

Hayek's main research theme was an important antidote to the most successful strains of thought in social sciences during the entire twentieth century. Hayek's foes were 'constructivist' thinkers who assumed that all social institutions are, and ought to be, the product of deliberate design. Hayek defied constructivism both in its factual and in its normative conclusions. Existing institutions are not all the product of human design, neither could it be possible to make the entire social order entirely dependent on a single mind's design, without undermining the possibilities of making the best of dispersed knowledge in society.

A Patron Saint for Anarchy?

In a short article in the *Libertarian Forum* (a little magazine authored and typewritten by himself almost from the first to the last line), Murray N. Rothbard came to rescue social Darwinism from a 'bad intellectual press,' obviously having Spencer in mind. The lesson of social Darwinists such as Spencer and William Graham Sumner was, after all, that 'the natural law of cause and effect works its inexorable way, and what this means is that bad premises, bad goals and ineffective means are dysfunctional for man' (1971a, p. 2). Therefore, libertarians could cheer up because 'the eventual victory of liberty is inevitable, because only liberty is functional for the modern man' (1971a, p. 3).

Rothbard was no fan of Hayek's evolutionary classical liberalism himself, and in fact he revamped a version of Lockean liberalism, focused on self-ownership as the basis of the natural right to property – and on the right to property as the basis of freedom in society. An economist by training, Rothbard was also a historian and a political thinker, and he was strongly impressed with the need to build a broader free-market movement, besides what in the United States was called the Old Right – the remnant of disciples of those intellectuals (Albert J. Nock among others) that in between the two wars opposed the Rooseveltian New Deal.

More than anybody else, Rothbard forged the contemporary libertarian movement. He blended together the tradition of natural law, Austrian economics, and the political non-interventionism of the American Old Right to produce a revised and – to his mind – more consistent version of classical liberalism. Rothbard burned many bridges in his path to consistency. He was an anarchist, and believed libertarians should not encourage middle of the road solutions. This separated him clearly from many contemporary libertarians, who are content with advocating a strict constitutional limitation of state duties or, in the United States, an allegiance to the old gospel of the Declaration of Independence.

Rothbard was well acquainted with Spencer – and in the Seventies he followed the development of the revival of interest in Spencer's works, as proved by a short but revealing review of Andreski (1972) and Peel (1971). Peel's work is deemed to be the output of a 'hopelessly confused and eclectic thinker' who cannot make sense of the 'unholy mess' of the 'science' of sociology and whose insights are vitiated by a form of 'extreme relativism and historicism.' Andreski (1972) on the contrary 'has the merit of taking Spencer's ideas seriously' but he too suffers from the original sin of being a sociologist and a 'middle-of-the-roader politically.' 'How superior is Spencer to his commentators!' laments Rothbard, who cherished Spencer's anti-militarism, his embrace of the industrial society and his defense of liberty, but who thought nonetheless that Spencer still needed 'a historian or biographer worthy of their subject' (Rothbard 1975, p. 3).

Like Leoni (2008), Rothbard contended that Spencer 'dared to believe in natural law and natural rights,' and therefore his methodology came to be unfashionable. This claim, as we saw, can be accepted only insofar as we understand that the laws of nature were very differently understood by Spencer than by authors such as Locke, to whom Rothbard looked far more for guidance.

Indeed, as Rothbard wrote for a strictly libertarian audience, despite the fact that 'Spencer more than any other figure was 'our' Marx,' he himself didn't make much of his legacy. Regardless of the difference between Spencer's and Hayek's evolutionism, Rothbard certainly showed some kind of congruence over many of Spencer's political positions – but, on a higher theoretical level, the affinities between the two are limited. They are similar in the sense their respective opuses are a very ambitious attempt to establish the philosophy of liberty on better grounds. We can search for Spencer's influence in Rothbard precisely because he was not content to be only an economist, but tried to construct a full bodied 'ethics of liberty.' Still, no matter how similar their goals could be, the pillars of Rothbard's worldview are not built with Spencerian bricks.

A serious scholar of Spencer's and active libertarian, George H. Smith, once expressed the hope that 'libertarians would do well to look at this phenomenal mind in their midst, and a necessary first step in placing Spencer in critical perspective is to revive his works and read it firsthand' (Smith 1999). Libertarians tend to agree that Spencer was 'unjustly neglected and often misrepresented' (Boaz 1997, p. 47) and they are happy, as is David Boaz, to add him to their canon (Boaz 1998). But the 'revival' of Spencer's works in libertarian circles seldom goes beyond some quotations in the blog circuits. George H. Smith's hope is yet to be fulfilled.

Towards a New Social Darwinism?

Partly in consequence of the influence of Hayek's work, the body of literature assessing economics in an evolutionary perspective is growing. Most of the authors involved in this intellectual enterprise do not make direct references to Spencer. What they do share, though, is an understanding of economics as an evolving order. In one way or another, these books all considered the market-based 'industrial' society as the output of a long cultural evolution. They try, in different ways, either to specify or complement this basic intuition, reading the evidence to explain how market arrangements were 'fit' to survive over time. The following list is by no means comprehensive.

Paul Seabright (2005) in his work explained how cooperation may be explained by institutions that brought human beings to treat the strangers as 'honorary friends.' In his book *Why Most Things Fail*, Paul Ormerod develops a theory based on the 'iron law of failure,' in which at any point in time each particular agent, be it a firm, a species or whatever, has its own level of fitness for survival. Those that fall below a critical value become extinct. By adding together the fitness levels of all the component parts, we can measure the fitness of the system as a whole and how it evolves over time. We see quite clearly that periods immediately following large extinctions tend to have relatively high overall fitness, as new firms are rushed in to fill the gaps opened up by the eliminations. In other words, extinctions essentially play the role Schumpeter describes with his phrase 'creative destruction.' Weaker firms are eliminated and replaced by firms that, on average, have higher levels of fitness (Ormerod 2005, p. 228).

Paul Rubin (2002) has developed a refined view of the economic extended order as a product of cultural evolution going back tens of centuries in our history as humankind. So did Larry Arnhart (1998 and 2005), whose 'Darwinian conservatism,' as the author admitted in an online article, 'looks a lot like' Spencer's evolutionary theory (Arnhart 2007). Arnhart dissociates his own 'Darwinian conservatism' from Spencer's politics stressing that he 'assumes a realist conception of human nature in which government will always be required to restrain human imperfection.' He seems thus to consider *Social Statics* as the ultimate political contribution of Spencer, assuming that it paved the way to anarchy.

Daniel Friedman (2008) has produced a brilliant primer in the evolutionary approach to economics – and mentions Spencer only in a footnote. Matt Ridley (2010) is perhaps the ultimate work in this stream of thought: a powerful and extremely insightful book on social evolution, free markets, and the reason for optimism in the future of humanity. Ridley comes from a scientific background – and, in the realm of economics, he refers to the insights of Hayek and of Nobel Laureate Vernon L. Smith, whose laboratory experiments have offered a new empirical grounding to the old truths of economics. He refers to Spencer just occasionally – though many of the points he raises (on the inadequacy of planning, on evolution and on complexity, for example) would be familiar to the Spencer reader.

An Author for Today?

A careful scholar of Spencer's such as Michael Taylor decreed that Spencer's work will remain 'a museum piece: an essential subject of study for those who wish to understand the Victorian age, but not the work of a major philosopher' (2007, p.152). There are many fields in which Spencer's *Synthetic Philosophy* is clearly outdated: advances in genetics, biology, physics and psychology contribute to emphasize that time doesn't pass in vain. To what extent Spencer's intuitions are still relevant is matter of debate.

Speaking of Spencer's political (ir)relevance, labelling Spencer a 'libertarian Marx' is hyperbolic at best. Clearly, there are parallels among the two: they were both system-builders, and they studied history to forecast what was to happen in the future, to name but the two most obvious ones. But perhaps one of the reason why Marx was *the* socialists' Marx, and Spencer wasn't the equivalent for classical liberals, is the fact that Marx's system is at the end of the day a critique of political economy and capitalism. As such, it can provide its followers with a political goal, without asking the far too ambitious request to embrace an all-encompassing world-view, ranging from physics to psychology. The dream of edifying a Marxist biology, a Marxist psychology, or a Marxist soccer for that matter, was the consequence of Marx being Marx, and the cause of that. By all means, being a Marxist is far more *economical* than trying to be a Spencerian.

To elucidate the motives for his neglect, we may further refer to an interesting case – that of England. The reader will pardon me if I oversimplify in condensing one hundred years of political history in a few lines.

The motherland of a vibrant classical liberal movement for two centuries, Britain became for most of the twentieth century the most socialistic country in the West. The New Liberal hegemony led a first wave of expansion of the scope of state's action, in the early 1900s. The focal point of the British welfare state, the National Health Service, bears the signature of 'liberal' Lord Beveridge (1879–1963). After the Second World War, the Labour Party fostered an aggressive program of nationalization. For most of this period, the Tories were – as they have been in Spencer's times and before – the party of the state.

The Thatcher government that rescued England from socialism was by and large influenced by the efforts of the Institute of Economic Affairs (IEA), a London-based think tank that

provided academics and journalists with a point of view consistently opposite to the then-dominant statist consensus. Led in its
glory days by Ralph Harris (1924–2006) and Arthur Seldon (1916–
2005), the Institute published a wide array of economists ranging from F. A. Hayek to James Buchanan – but never dug deeper
enough into the British liberal tradition to rediscover Spencer's
name.

This was probably for at least two very understandable reasons. The first is that for people engaged in the staggering
mission of reviving the good name of free enterprise in the age
of statism, associating themselves with social Darwinism was
clearly not the best advertising. Both Harris and Seldon came
from a modest family, and they both wisely made a point of
stressing that preaching the free market was not the equivalent
of glorifying capitalists. Spencer was never close to that, as we
saw, but the sticky label of social Darwinism made many believe
he did.

The second reason, is that – like most of think tanks, right or
left – the IEA privileged an *empirical* approach, focusing on efficient means to realize social goals, rather than promoting a
political philosophy per se.[3] The IEA has been true to Spencer's
prophecy: the goal of true liberals, in the twentieth century,
indeed proved to be countervailing the 'divine will' of democratically elected parliaments, and the right instruments to do
that were to be found in the arid toolbox of economics, more
than in the art gallery of political philosophy.

Is there a reason Spencer should be any more interesting
today? A reason can be found in the development of interest in
an evolutionary theory of society and the marketplace, that makes
liberty its political cornerstone and the relaxing of state regulation, its main policy prescription. This description mixes up, in
Spencerian fashion, the normative with the positive: but it fits the
outline of some of the works briefly described in this chapter.

Most of those works would have their patron saint in Friedrich
von Hayek. But, as polemically noted by the now arch-anti-
liberal John Gray in reviewing Matt Ridley's *The Rational Optimist*

(Gray 2010), they may be unintentionally resurrecting Herbert Spencer's thinking – at least in part. Evolution may prove to be an avenging god indeed.

Notes

[1] In one of the best books on Hayek's thought, Jeremy Shearmur noted passim that *The Sensory Order* 'in some ways resembles the "evolutionary" views on perception of Herbert Spencer' (Shearmur 1996, p. 234 n).

[2] See Hayek 1973, pp. 36–52.

[3] The Libertarian Alliance, a smaller group founded by Chris Tame, exhibited much more of an allegiance to Spencer's thought – but indeed its historical mission was more to aggregate people already sharing a libertarian philosophy, than to have an impact on the policy world.

Bibliography

Notes

As it was repeated a number of times in this volume, Herbert Spencer's body of work is vast and impressive to the extent of being intimidating. An occasional reader of Spencer's can surely benefit from reading *The Proper Sphere of Government* and *Man Versus the State*: they can be understood as the two poles between which Spencer develops his political thought and have been conveniently reprinted by the Liberty Fund of Indianapolis in a single volume, together with some of Spencer's most stimulating political works.

John Offer has put together highly relevant critical writings on Spencer, *Herbert Spencer: Critical Assessments* (2000), which require reading for a better appreciation of Spencer's political theory, as does Taylor's *Men Versus the State: Herbert Spencer and the Late Victorian Individualism* (1992), by far the best work available on Herbert Spencer and the individualist movement in Britain.

Nisbet places Spencer in the 'history of the idea of progress.' By reading this work, *History of the Idea of Progress* (1980), you'll catch two birds with one stone: you'll be introduced to Spencer's as well as to Nisbet's ideas, with the latter's insights proving truly instrumental in so 'small' an effort as making sense of the modern world.

The historian and the specialist may go further. *Social Statics* is a rewarding read, though it necessitates some effort to properly contextualized. *Political Institutions* is required to achieve a proper understanding of Spencer's sociology. Among the writings of his followers, Auberon Herbert's *The Right and Wrong of Compulsion by the State and Other Essays*, reprinted by the Liberty Fund in 1978, is unparalleled in conveying a sense of what Spencerian individualism was.

Among recent critical works, Peel (*Herbert Spencer: The Evolution of a Sociologist*, 1971) is illuminating and full of insights. Gray (*The Political Philosophy of Herbert Spencer: Individualism and Organicism*, 1996) is helpful for a better comprehension of the tensions in Spencer's thinking. Wiltshire (*The Social and Political Thought of Herbert Spencer*, 1978) and Weinstein (*Equal Freedom and Utility: Herbert Spencer's Liberal Utilitarianism*, 1998) are important attempts in finding the proper place for Spencer in the world of political ideas. Francis (*Herbert Spencer and the Invention of Modern Life*, 2007) is a most interesting and detailed biographical work on Spencer. Taylor (*The Philosophy of Herbert Spencer*, 2007) provides a comprehensive introduction to the *Synthetic Philosophy*. Though some of the conclusions of these works are not shared by the present author, they are clearly now part of the Spencerian canon.

The 1982 special issue of *History of Political Thought* reunites some of the most challenging and intriguing contemporary comments on Spencer – most of which are reprinted in Offer (Herbert Spencer: *Critical Assessments* 2000). Hofstadter's (*Social Darwinism in American Thought* (1992) is and shall remain a controversial classic on social Darwinism inasmuch as its conclusions have polluted the public debate on evolutionary theory. However, it is a wonderful book that would benefit any critical reader – history of ideas at its best – and as such inevitably entails political passion.

Most of Spencer's writings are now available through the Online Library of Liberty, a project of the Liberty Fund which can never be praised enough. If, in your busy life, you have time to read but one of Spencer's essays, I would defer to the authority of Robert Nisbet and recommend the reading of 'Overlegislation,' now available online. It is a Spencer classic that speaks as much to the world of Barack Obama as to that of William Gladstone and Benjamin Disraeli.

Works by Herbert Spencer
(Listed in Order of Original Publication)

The Proper Sphere of Government (1843), now in 1981.

Social Statics (1851), New York: Robert Schalkenbach Foundation, 1995.

'A Theory of Population Deduced from the General Law of Animal Fertility' (1852a) *Westminster Review.*

'The Developmental Hypothesis' (1852b), in *Essays: Scientific, Political, and Speculative*, vol. I. London: Williams and Norgate, 1891.

'OverLegislation' (1853), now in 1981.

'Railways Morals and Railways Policy' (1854), in *Essays: Scientific, Political, and Speculative*, vol. III. London: Williams and Norgate, 1891.

Principles of Psychology (1855a). London: Longman, Brown, Green and Longmans.

'What Knowledge is of Most Worth?' (1855b), in 1911.

'Progress: Its Law and Cause' (1857), in *Essays: Scientific, Political, and Speculative*, vol. I. London: Williams and Norgate, 1891.

'State-tamperings with Money and Banks' (1858), in Essays: Scientific, Political, and Speculative, vol. III. London: Williams and Norgate, 1891.

'The Morals of Trade' (1859), in *Essays: Scientific, Political, and Speculative*, vol. III. London: Williams and Norgate, 1891.

'The Social Organism' (1860), in *Essays: Scientific, Political, and Speculative*, vol. I. London: Williams and Norgate, 1891.

First Principles (1862), London: Williams and Norgate. 1915.

'Reasons for Dissenting from the Philosophy of M. Comte' (1862), in *Essays: Scientific, Political, and Speculative*, vol. II. London: Williams and Norgate, 1891.

The Principles of Biology, 2 vols., London, Williams & Norgate, 1864, 1867.

Social Statics (1868), New York: Appleton.

'Specialized Administration' (1871), now in 1981.

The Study of Sociology (1873), London: King.

Political Institutions, being Part V of the Principles of Sociology (1882) (The Concluding Portion of Vol. II). London: Williams and Norgate.

'The Americans: A Conversation and a Speech, with an Addition' (1883), in Essays: Scientific, Political, and Speculative, vol. III. London: Williams and Norgate, 1891.

The Man Versus the State (1884), now in 1981.

'M. de Laveleye's Error' (1885), in *Various Fragments*. New York: Appleton, 1910.

'From Freedom to Bondage' (1891), now in Mackay 1981.

The Principles of Ethics (1893), 2 vols. Indianapolis: Liberty Fund, 1978.

'Evolutionary Ethics' (1898), in *Various Fragments*. New York: Appleton, 1910.

'The Filiation of Ideas' (1899), now in Duncan, D. (1908), vol. II.

Facts and Comments (1902), New York: Appleton.

An Autobiography (1904), 2 vols. London: Williams and Norgate.

Essays on Education and Kindred Subjects (1911), London: J. M. Dent and Sons, Ltd., 1983.

Man Versus the State With Six Essays on Government, Society, and Freedom (1981), Indianapolis: Liberty Fund.

Duncan, D., *Life and Letters of Herbert Spencer* (1908), 2 vols. New York: Appleton.

Secondary Literature

Adcock, R. (2009), 'Rethinking Classical Liberalism in "Progressive" Times: The Divergent Sociologies of Spencer and Sumner,' Paper presented at the Annual Meeting of the American Political Science Association, Toronto.

Andreski, S. (ed.) (1972), *Herbert Spencer: Structure, Function and Evolution.* London: Joseph.

Arnhart, L. (2007), 'Herbert Spencer's Utopian Anarchism,' available here: darwinianconservatism.blogspot.com/2007/01/herber-spencers-utopian-anarchism.htm.

Blanchard, J. U. (1984), 'Exclusive Interview with F. A. Hayek,' *Cato Policy Report*, VI, 3.

Burrow, J. W. (1966), *Evolution and Society: A Study in Victorian Social Theory.* Cambridge: Cambridge University Press.

Carneiro, R. L. (1981), 'Herbert Spencer as an Anthropologist,' *The Journal of Libertarian Studies*, 5, 2.

Elwick, J. (2003), 'Herbert Spencer and the Disunity of the Social Organism,' *History of Science*, 41.

Ferri, E. (1909), *Socialism and Positive Science (Darwin-Spencer-Marx).* London: Independent Labour Party.

Francis, M. (1978), 'Herbert Spencer and the myth of laissez-faire,' Journal of the History of Ideas, 39, 2.

—(2007), *Herbert Spencer and the Invention of Modern Life.* Stockfield: Acumen.

Frankel Paul, E. (1983), 'Herbert Spencer: The Historicist as a Failed Prophet,' *Journal of the History of Ideas*, 44, 4.

George, H. (1879), Progress and Poverty, New York: Webster.

—(1892), *A Perplexed Philosopher: Being an Examination of Herbert Spencer's Various Utterances on the Land Question, with Some Incidental Reference to His Synthetic Philosophy*, New York: Webster.

Gray, J. (1982), 'Spencer on the Ethics of Liberty,' *History of Political Thought*, 3, 3.

Gray, T. S. (1996), *The Political Philosophy of Herbert Spencer: Individualism and Organicism*. Aldershot: Avebury.

Herbert, A. (1906), 'Mr. Spencer and the Great Machine,' now in A. Herbert, *The Right and Wrong of Compulsion by the State and Other Essays*.

Hofstadter, R. (1992), *Social Darwinism in American Thought* (1944). Boston: Beacon Press.

Huxley, T. (1891), 'Administrative Nihilism' (1871), in *Method and Result: Collected Essays Part One*. London: Macmillan.

Machan, T. (1978), 'Introduction' to Herbert Spencer, *The Principles of Ethics*.

Mackay, T. (ed.) (1981), *A Plea for Liberty: An Argument against Socialism and Socialistic Legislation, consisting of an Introduction by Herbert Spencer and Essays by Various Writers* (1891). Indianapolis: Liberty Fund.

Maitland, F. W. (1911), 'Mr. Herbert Spencer's Theory of Society' (1883), in *The Collected Papers of Frederic William Maitland*. Cambridge: Cambridge University Press.

McCann, C. R., Jr (2004), *Individualism and the Social Order: The Social Element in Liberal Thought*. London: Routledge.

Meadowcroft, John (1995), *Conceptualizing the State Innovation and Dispute in British Political Thought 1880–1914*. Oxford: Clarendon Press.

Miller, W. L. (1982), 'Spencer's Drift to Conservatism,' *History of Political Thought*, 3, 3.

Nock, A. J. (1981), 'Introduction' to Spencer 1981.

Offer, J. (ed.) (2000), *Herbert Spencer: Critical Assessments*, 4 vols. London: Routledge.

Paul, J. (1982), 'The Socialism of Herbert Spencer,' *History of Political Thought*, 3, 3.

Peel, J. D. Y. (1971), Herbert Spencer: *The Evolution of a Sociologist*. New York: Basic Books.

Perrin, R. G. (1963), *Herbert Spencer. A Primary and Secondary Bibliography*. New York: Garland.

Roark, E. (2004), 'Herbert Spencer's Evolutionary Individualism,' *Quarterly Journal of Ideology*, 27, 3–4.

Rothbard. M. N. (1971), 'Social Darwinism Reconsidered,' *Libertarian Forum*, 3, 1, http://mises.org/journals/libertarianforum.asp

—(1975), 'Herbert Spencer. Structure, Function and Evolution – Herbert Spencer: The Evolution of a Sociologist,' Libertarian Review, 4, 8, http://www.libertarianism.org/lr/index.html

Smith, G. H. (1978), 'Will the Real Herbert Spencer Please Stand Up?,' now in Id (1999), *Atheism, Ayn Rand, and Other Heresies*. New York: Prometheus.

—(1981), 'Herbert Spencer's Theory of Causation,' *The Journal of Libertarian Studies*, 5, 2.

Steiner, H. (1982), 'Land, Liberty and the Early Spencer,' *History of Political Thought*, 3, 3.

Taylor, M. W. (1989), 'The Errors of an Evolutionist: a Reply to Ellen Frankel Paul,' *Political Studies*, 37, 3.

—(1992), *Men Versus the State: Herbert Spencer and the Late Victorian Individualism*. Oxford: Oxford University Press.

—(1996), 'Introduction' to Taylor, M. W. (ed.), *Herbert Spencer and the Limits of the State: The Late Nineteenth-century Debate between Individualism and Collectivism*. Bristol: Thoemmes Press.

—(2007), *The Philosophy of Herbert Spencer*. New York: Continuum.

Turner, J. H. (1985), *Herbert Spencer: a Renewed Appreciation*. Beverly Hills: Sage.

Weinstein, D. (1998), *Equal Freedom and Utility: Herbert Spencer's Liberal Utilitarianism*. Cambridge: Cambridge University Press.

Wiltshire, D. (1978), *The Social and Political Thought of Herbert Spencer*. Oxford: Oxford University Press.

Works of General Interest

Arnhart, L. (1998), *Darwinian Natural Rights: The Biological Ethics of Human Nature*. New York: State University of New York.

—(2005), *Darwinian Conservatism*. Exeter: Imprint.

—(2007), 'Herbert Spencer's Utopian Anarchism,' available at http:// darwinianconservatism.blogspot.com.

Barker, R. (1997), *Political Ideas in Modern Britain: In and After the 20th Century*, second edition. London: Routledge.

Barnes, H. E. (1924), *Sociology and Political Theory: A Consideration of the Sociological Basis of Politics*. New York: Knopf.

Barnett, R. E. (1977), 'Whither Anarchy? Has Robert Nozick Justified the State?,' *Journal of Libertarian Studies*, 1.

—(1998), *The Structure of Liberty. Justice and the Rule of Law*. Oxford: Clarendon Press.

Barton, R. (1998), 'Huxley, Lubbock and Half a Dozen Others: Professionals and Gentlemen in the Formation of the X Club, 1851–1964,' *Isis*, 89, 3.

Biagini, E. F. (1992), *Liberty, Retrenchment and Reform: Popular Liberalism in the Age of Gladstone, 1860–1880*. Cambridge: Cambridge University Press.

Blanchard, J. U. (1984), 'Exclusive Interview with F.A. Hayek,' Cato Policy Report, VI, 3.

Boaz, D. (1997), *Libertarianism: A Primer*. New York: Free Press.

Boaz, D. (ed.) (1998), *The Libertarian Reader: Classic and Contemporary Writings from Lao Tzu to Milton Friedman*. New York: Free Press.

Brinton, C. (1949), *English Political Thought in the Nineteenth Century* (1933). Cambridge: Harvard University Press.

Brown, D. (2006), *Richard Hofstadter. An Intellectual Biography*. Chicago: University of Chicago Press.

Brozen, Y. (1965), 'The Revival of Traditional Liberalism,' *New Individualist Review*, 3, 4.

Burke, E. (1999), Selected Works of Edmund Burke. Vol. I. Thoughts on the Present Discontents. Two Speeches on America, Indianapolis: Liberty Fund.

Capaldi, N. (2004), *John Stuart Mill: A Biography*. Cambridge: Cambridge University Press.

Casson, M., and Godley, A. (2010), 'Entrepreneurship in Britain, 1830–1900,' in Landes D., Mokyr J., and William Baumol, *The Invention of Enterprise: Entrepreneurship from Ancient Mesopotamia to Modern Times*, Princeton: Princeton University Press.

Channon, G. (1999), 'The Business Morals of British Railway Companies in the Mid-Nineteenth Century,' *Business and Economic History*, 28, 2.

Childs, R. A. Jr (1977), 'The Invisible Hand Strikes Back,' *Journal of Libertarian Studies*, 1, 1.

Cohen, G. A. (1995), *Self-Ownership, Freedom and Equality*. Cambridge: Cambridge University Press.

Constant, B. (1819), The Liberty of the Ancient Compared with That of the Moderns, now in Id, Political Writings, Cambridge: Cambridge University Press, 1988.

Conway, D. (1995), Classical Liberalism: The Unvanquished Ideal, London: Macmillan.

Dicey, A. V. (1905), *Lectures on the Relation between Law and Public Opinion in England: During the Nineteenth Century*. London: MacMillan.

Dixon Davidson, C. (1892), 'Relations between Parents and Children,' *Liberty, September*.

Doherty, B. (2007), *Radicals for Capitalism: A Freewheeling History of the Modern American Libertarian Movement*. New York: Public Affairs.

Donisthorpe, W. (1894), *Individualism: A System of Politics*. London: MacMillan.

Durkheim, E. (1964), *The Division of Labour in Society* (1893), New York, Free Press.

Easterbrook, F. H., and D. R. Fischel (1991), 'Limited Liability and the Corporation,' *University of Chicago Law Review* 52, 1.

Edwards, R. D. (1993), *The Pursuit of Reason. The Economist 1843–1993*. London: Hamish Hamilton.

Ekelund, R. B., and R. D. Tollison (1997), *Politicized Economies: Monarchy, Monopoly, and Mercantilism*, Austin: Texas A&M University Press.

Ekirch, A. (2009), *The Decline of American Liberalism* (1955). Oakland CA: The Independent Institute.

Epstein North, D. (1985), *The Apprenticeship of Beatrice Webb*. Amherst: University of Massachusetts Press.

Frankel, Paul E. (1980), 'Laissez Faire in Nineteenth-Century Britain: Fact or Myth?' *Literature of Liberty*, 3, 4.

Freeden, M. (1978), *The New Liberalism: An Ideology of Social Reform*. Oxford: Clarendon Press.

Friedman, D. (2008), *Morals and Markets: An Evolutionary Account of the Modern World*. London: Palgrave.

Gamble, A. (1996), Hayek. The Iron Cage of Liberty, Boulder, CO: Westview Press.

Gillman, M., and T. Eade (1995), 'The Development of the Corporation in England, with Emphasis on Limited Liability,' *International Journal of Social Economics*, 22, 4.

Goschen, G. J. (1885), 'Since 1880,' *Nineteenth Century*, 17.

Gray, J. (1998), *Hayek on Liberty* (1984). London: Blackwell.

—(2010), 'The Rational Optimist: How Prosperity Evolves,' *New Statesman*, http://www.newstatesman.com/books/2010/08/ridley-climate-evolution-ideas.

Green, T. H. (1888), 'Lecture on liberal legislation and freedom of contract' (1881), in id., *The Works of Thomas Hill Green*, vol. III. London: Longmans.

—(1986), *Lectures on the Principles of Political Obligation* (1883). Cambridge: Cambridge University Press.

Halevy, E. (1956), *Thomas Hodgskin* (1905), translated and edited by A. J. Taylor. London: Ernst Benn.

—(1966), *The Growth of Philosophic Radicalism* (1904). Boston: Beacon Press.

Hamowy, R. (1987), *The Scottish Enlightenment and the Theory of Spontaneous Order*. Carbondale: Southern Illinois University Press.

Hamowy, R., and W. F. Buckely (1961), 'National Review: Criticism and Reply,' *New Individualist Review*, 1, 3.

Harris, R. (2000), Industrializing English Law: Entrepreneurship and Business Organization, 1720–1844, Cambridge: Cambridge University Press.

Hawkins, M. (2003), *Social Darwinism in European and American Thought 1860–1945: Nature as Model and Nature as Threat.* Cambridge: Cambridge University Press.

Hayek, F. A. von (1945), 'The Use of Knowledge in Society,' *American Economic Review*, 35, 4.

—(1960a), *The Constitution of Liberty*, Chicago: University of Chicago Press.

—(1960b), The Sensory Order: An Inquiry into the Foundations of Theoretical Psychology, Chicago: University of Chicago Press.

—(1967), 'Notes on the Evolution of Systems of Rules of Conduct,' in id., *Studies in Philosophy, Politics, and Economics.* Chicago: University of Chicago Press.

—(1973), *Law, Legislation, and Liberty: Rules and Order*, Chicago: University of Chicago Press.

—(1979), Law, Legislation and Liberty: The Political Order of a Free People, Chicago: University of Chicago Press.

Herbert, A. (1884), 'A Politician in Sight of Haven,' in *The Right and Wrong of Compulsion by the State and Other Essays.* Indianapolis: Liberty Fund, 1978.

—(1885) 'The Right and Wrong of Compulsion by the State' (1885), in *The Right and Wrong of Compulsion by the State and Other Essays.* Indianapolis: Liberty Fund, 1978.

—(1894), 'The Ethics of Dynamite' (1894), in *The Right and Wrong of Compulsion by the State and Other Essays.* Indianapolis: Liberty Fund, 1978.

—(1906), 'Mr. Spencer and the Great Machine,' in *The Right and Wrong of Compulsion by the State and Other Essays.* Indianapolis: Liberty Fund, 1978.

Himmelfarb, G. (1959), *Darwin and the Darwninian Revolution.* New York: Doubleday.

—(1992), *Poverty and Compassion. The Moral Imagination of Late Victorians.* New York: Vintage.

—(2004), *The Road to Modernity. The British, French and American Enlightenments.* New York: Knopf.

Hobhouse, L. T. (1971), *Liberalism* (1911). Oxford: Oxford University Press.

—(1913), *Development and Purpose: An Essay Towards a Philosophy of Evolution.* London: MacMillan.

Hobson, J. A. (1898), 'Rich Man's Anarchism,' *The Humanitarian*, 1, 12, and in Taylor (ed.), *Herbert Spencer and the Limits of the State.*

—(1902), *Imperialism: A Study*. New York: James Pott.

—(1909), The Crisis of Liberalism: New Issues of Democracy. London: P. S. King and Son.

Hodgskin, T. (1832), The Natural and Artificial Right of Property Contrasted, London: Steil.

Hoppe, H. H. (2001), 'Anarcho-Capitalism: An Annotated Bibliography,' in *LewRockwell.com*, http: //www.lewrockwell.com/hoppe/hoppe5. html.

Huerta de Soto, J. (2009), 'Classical Liberalism versus Anarcho-Capitalism,' in Jörg Guido Hülsmann and Stephan Kinsella (eds) , *Property, Freedom, Society: Essays in Honor of Hans-Hermann Hoppe*. Auburn, AL: Ludwig von Mises Institute.

Humboldt, W. von (1993), *The Limits of State Action* (1791). Indianapolis: Liberty Fund.

Hutchison, T. W. (1978), *On Revolutions and Progress in Economic Knowledge*. Cambridge: Cambridge University Press.

Infantino, L. (1998), *Individualism in Modern Thought: From Adam Smith to Hayek*. London: Routledge.

Keynes, J. M. (1972), 'The End of Laissez-Faire' (1926), in *Essays in Persuasion*. Cambridge: Cambridge University Press.

La Vergata, A. (1995), 'Herbert Spencer: Biology, Sociology and Cosmic Evolution,' in Leoni, B. (2008), *Il pensiero politico contemporaneo*. Macerata: Liberilibri.

Maasen, S., E. Mendelsohn, and P. Weingast (eds.), *Biology as Society, Society as Biology: Metaphors*. Dontrecht: Kluwer.

Macey, J. (2009), Corporate Governance: Promises made, Promises Broken, New Haven: Yale University Press.

Mack, E. (1978), 'Voluntaryism: The Political Thought of Auberon Herbert,' *Journal of Libertarian Studies*, 2, 4.

Maine, H. (1905), *Ancient Law: Its Connection with the Early History of Society and Its Relation to Modern Ideas* (1861). London: Routledge.

McCloskey, D. (2006), *The Bourgeois Virtues: Ethics for an Age of Commerce*. Chicago: University of Chicago Press.

Meadowcroft, John, (1996), 'Introduction' to John Meadowcroft (ed.), *The Liberal Political Tradition: Contemporary Reappraisals*. Chaltham: Elgar.

—(2005), *The Ethics of the Market*. New York: Palgrave MacMillan.

Miller, D. (1976), Social Justice, Oxford: Clarendon Press.

Molinari, G. de (1977), *The Production of Security* (1849). New York: Center for Libertarian Studies.

Muthu, S. (1999), *Enlightenment Against Empire*, Princeton: Princeton University Press.

—(2008), 'Theorizing "Globalization" in the Age of Enlightenment: Adam Smith's Critique of International Trading Companies,' *Political Theory*, 36, 2.

Nisbet, R. (1980), *History of the Idea of Progress.* New York: Basic Books.

Nock, A. J. (1935), *Our Enemy, the State.* New York: Murro and Sons.

Nozick, R. (1974), *Anarchy, State and Utopia.* New York: Basic Books.

Ormerod, P. (2005), *Why Most Things Fail: Evolution, Extinction and Economics.* Hoboken: Wiley.

Otsuka, M. (2003), *Libertarianism without Inequality.* Oxford: Oxford University Press.

Pareto, V. (1966), 'L'avvenire dell'Europa: il punto di vista di un italiano' (1922), in *Scritti sociologici minori.* Torino: Utet.

Parsons T. (1937), *The Structure of Social Action.* New York: McGraw Hill.

Paul, D. (2009), 'Darwin, Social Darwinism and Eugenics,' in J. Hodge, and G. Radic (eds.), *The Cambridge Companion to Darwin.* Cambridge: Cambridge University Press.

Raico, R. (1995), "Austrian Economics and Classical Liberalism", *Advances in Austrian Economics*, 2A, 1995.

Ridley, M. (2010), *The Rational Optimist: How Prosperity Evolves.* New York: HarperCollins.

Rogers, J. E. T. (ed.) (1873), *Cobden and Modern Political Opinion: Essays on Certain Political Topics.* London: Macmillan.

Rothbard, M. N. (1968), 'Confessions of a Right-Wing Liberal,' *Ramparts*, 6, 4, http://www.lewrockwell.com/rothbard/rothbard77.html.

—(1970), *Power and Market, Government and the Economy*, Menlo Park, CA: Institute for Humane Studies.

—(1977), 'Robert Nozick and the Immaculate Conception of the State,' *Journal of Libertarian Studies*, 1.

—(2009), 'Confidential Memo on F. A. Hayek's Constitution of Liberty' (1958), in id., *Murray N. Rothbard vs. the Philosophers: Unpublished Writings on Hayek, Mises, Strauss and Polanyi.* Auburn, AL: Ludwig von Mises Institute.

Rubin, P. H. (2002), *Darwinian Politics: The Evolutionary Origin of Freedom.* New Brunswick: Rutgers University Press.

Russell, B. (2004), *History of Western Philosophy* (1945). London: Routledge.

Schumpeter, J. (1954), *Capitalism, Socialism and Democracy*, London: George Allen & Unwin.

Seabright, P. (2005), *The Company of Strangers: A Natural History of Economic Life.* Princeton: Princeton University Press.

Shaw, G. B. (1921), *Ruskin's Politics.* London: Ruskin Centenary Council.

Shearmur, J. (1996), *Hayek and After: Hayekian Liberalism as a Research Programme*. London: Routledge.

Sidgwick, H. (1899), 'The Relation of Ethics to Sociology,' *International Journal of Ethics*, 10.

Smith, A. (1937), *An Inquiry into Nature and Causes of the Wealth of Nations* (1776), ed. Edwin Cannan. New York: Random House.

Smith, V. C. (1990), *The Rationale of Central Banking and the Free Banking Alternative*, (1836). Indianapolis: Liberty Fund.

Spinner, T. J. (1973), *George Joachim Goschen: The Transformation of a Victorian Liberal*. Cambridge: Cambridge University Press.

Stack, D. (1998), *Nature and Artifice, The Life and Thought of Thomas Hodgskin, 1787–1869*. Suffolck: Boydel Press.

Stigler, G. J. (1975), 'The Intellectual and His Society,' in Richard T. Selden (ed.), *Capitalism and Freedom: Problems and Prospects*. Charlottesville: University Press of Virginia.

Sumner, W. G. (1881), 'Sociology,' in Sumner 1919.

—(1883), 'The Forgotten Man,' in Sumner 1918.

—(1886), 'What is Free Trade,' in Sumner 1918.

—(1888), *Protectionism. The -ism Which Teaches that Waste Makes Wealth*. New York: Holt.

—(1898), 'The Conquest of the United States by Spain,' in Sumner 1919.

—(1903), 'War,' in Sumner 1919.

—(1914), 'The Challenge of Facts,' in A. G. Keller (ed.), *The Challenge of Facts and Other Essays*. New Haven: Yale University Press.

—(1918), *The Forgotten Man and Other Essays*, ed. A. G. Keller. New Haven: Yale University Press.

—(1919), *War and Other Essays*, ed. A. G. Keller. New Haven: Yale University Press.

—(2007), *What Social Classes Owe to Each Other* (1883). Charleston: BiblioBazar.

Tame, C. (1980), 'The Libertarian Tradition No.1: Auberon Herbert,' *Free Life, The Journal of the Libertarian Alliance*, 1, 2.

Trask, H. A. S. (2004), 'William Graham Sumner: Against Democracy, Plutocracy and Imperialism,' *Journal of Libertarian Studies*, 18, 4.

Trentmann, F. (2008), *Free Trade Nation. Commerce, Consumption and Civil Society in Modern Britain*. Oxford: Oxford University Press.

Turney-High, H. (1937), *Primitive War: Its Theory and Concepts*. Columbia: University of South Carolina Press.

Vallentyne, P. and Hillel Steiner (eds) (2000), *Left-Libertarianism and Its Critics*. Basingstoke: Palgrave.

Van Creveld, M. (1999), *The Rise and Decline of the State*. Cambridge: Cambridge University Press.

Watner, C. (1986), 'The English Individualists as They Appear in Liberty,' in M. E. Coughlin, C. H. Hamilton, and M. A. Sullivan (eds), *Benjamin R. Tucker and The Champions of Liberty: A Centenary Anthology*. New York: Coughlin and Sullivan.

Webb, B. (1979), *My Apprenticeship* (1926). Cambridge: Press Syndicate of the University of Cambridge.

Webb, S., and B. Webb (1911), *The History of Trade Unionism*. London: The Fabian Society.

Werth, B. (2009), *Banquet at Dalmonico's: Great Minds, the Gilded Age, and the Triumph of Evolution in America*. New York: Random House.

Zagorin, P. (2003), *How the Idea of Religious Toleration Came to the West*, Princeton: Princeton University Press.

Index